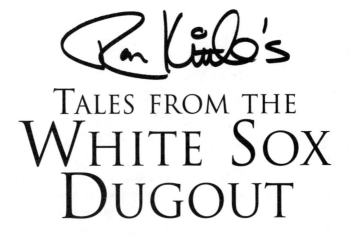

Ron Kittle's
TALES FROM THE
WHITE SOX
DUGOUT

RON KITTLE
WITH BOB LOGAN

FOREWORD BY ROLAND HEMOND

www.SportsPublishingLLC.com

ISBN: 1-58261-543-8

Publishers: Peter L. Bannon and Joseph J. Bannon Sr.
Senior managing editor: Susan M. Moyer
Acquisitions editor: Scott Musgrave
Developmental editor: Noah Adams Amstadter
Art director: K. Jeffrey Higgerson
Dust jacket design: Joseph Brumleve
Project manager: Kathryn R. Holleman
Imaging: Dustin Hubbart, Heidi Norsen, and
        Kenneth J. O'Brien
Photo editor: Erin Linden-Levy

Printed in the United States of America

Sports Publishing L.L.C.
804 North Neil Street
Champaign, IL 61820

Phone: 1-877-424-2665
Fax: 217-363-2073
Web site: www.SportsPublishingLLC.com

For my wife, Laurie, and my children, Hayley and Dylan, and the rest of my family and friends for their continued support through the good swings and bad swings and many ups and downs of my career. And to the late James W. Kittle, my father, for never letting me forget where I came from and how hard I had to work to just be a little above average. And to the wonderful people I have met through my years in baseball—they will never be forgotten.

—R.K.

Some of the best times in my 40-plus years covering Chicago sports were spent on the South Side, trying to figure out what the White Sox were up—or down—to. I'm glad that Jerry Reinsdorf and Eddie Einhorn kept alive the unbroken tradition of American League baseball in this toddlin' town. Thanks to Nancy Faust, who made Sox fans bellow "Yes! Yes!" to "Na, Na" with her marvelous music, and to Roland Hemond and Bob Grim, a couple of all-around good guys.

—B.L.

CONTENTS

FOREWORD

Note: Roland Hemond long ago proved the exception to Leo Durocher's adage "Nice guys finish last." Hemond is one of baseball's certified Good Guys and sharpest minds. He was general manager of the Chicago White Sox in 1983 and deserves much of the credit for building a team that confounded the experts when it won and had fun, all in the same season.

Fun really was the signature of the 1983 White Sox. They got together on the road, not just to talk baseball, but to have some laughs. Jerry Koosman was a major factor in keeping everybody loose. So was Greg Luzinski, with his dry sense of humor. Marc Hill was the resident clubhouse prankster, ably assisted by Tom Paciorek and Dennis Lamp. The quiet guys, like Harold Baines and Vance Law, didn't add much to the frivolity, but they shared the enjoyment with a club where everybody got along, including Manager Tony La Russa and his outstanding coaches.

Ron Kittle was one of the best at having fun, especially for a rookie. He looked like he'd been around forever, even though '83 was his first full year in the majors. Ron's refreshing personality and ability to deliver big hits in the clutch played a huge role in the way the White Sox were able to shake off a slow start and come on strong to win their division by 20 games.

Most fans still are unaware of what Kittle went through to make his big-league dream come true. He showed me real courage and perseverance in overcoming spinal surgery and other injuries to earn a second chance with the White Sox, after being told he'd never play baseball again. For me, the biggest thrill of the 1983 All-Star game was the fabulous standing ovation Ron got from that jam-packed Comiskey Park crowd. I'm pleased that Ron Kittle and Bob Logan, one of Chicago's most respected sportswriters, have combined to tell this story of a player and a team that wouldn't quit.

—ROLAND HEMOND

PREFACE

On the morning of October 2, 1982, I was a sleepy *Chicago Tribune* sportswriter, starting an unusual day in the inflated gasbag known to Minneapolis fans as the Hubert H. Humphrey Metrodome. Bears coach Mike Ditka later hung a better label on this sorry excuse for a big-league stadium—the Rollerdome.

The White Sox had been sentenced to play the Twins in a rare morning baseball game there, because Illinois and Minnesota were to renew their Big Ten football rivalry that evening on the same turf.

Little did I suspect that a memorable moment in Chicago sports history would enliven the otherwise forgettable Sox-Twins clash. A Sox rookie named Ron Kittle launched his first big-league homer off Twins' ace Frank Viola. I don't even remember who won the game, but before long, this intriguing newcomer led first the South Side and then all of Chicago toward an electric, if totally unexpected, ride to a spot fans hadn't glimpsed for years—the winner's circle.

Kittle's ability to blend baseball-bashing power with charismatic charm soon took the Windy City by storm. He emerged as a notable, quotable member of the 1983 Sox team that splashed the words "Winnin' Ugly" across our sports pages in bold headlines. The youngster from Northwest Indiana became an overnight sensation, joshing about his towering homers atop Comiskey Park's roof with a brand of self-deprecating humor, soon dubbed "Kittleisms," that made him a media and fan favorite.

Along with everybody else, except opposing pitchers, I savored Kitty's meteoric rise to stardom, because he had fun playing baseball and made it equally enjoyable to watch and write about. Not until now, when Ron asked me to help tell tales from his remarkable career in this book, did I begin to understand the price he paid for fame. It's an American success story that I believe should be read by every boy or girl with a dream.

—BOB LOGAN

1

HARD ROAD
TO THE TOP
It Takes Iron Will, Plus Skill

ALL IN THE FAMILY

It's true I always thought I could do better if I worked a little harder. That unquenchable spirit, if that's what you want to call it, came from my Dad, James "Slim" Kittle. He pushed himself to the limit every day on the job until he was as hard as the iron and steel he worked with. With him, there were no excuses. The way he brought all of us kids up, there was no chance I could accept failure. I think I did it more for him than for myself, but I was not going to let an injury stand in my way.

NO SOFT TOUCHES

It never occurred to me to raise my hand to my dad, even though all of us kids got some severe whippings when we were younger. Nowadays, it probably would be considered child abuse. Finally, when I was a senior in high school, I wrecked his car accidentally, and I thought he was going to backhand me or punch me. I grabbed his hand, because I wasn't going to let that happen anymore. I want to make it clear that my dad was not a bad man. We respected him, and he wanted us to be disciplined kids.

Work was the first priority for the Kittles, but I found time to play baseball, football and basketball, ride my bike and do the things most kids did in that much more innocent world I grew up in. But while my friends were hanging out on Miller Beach by the Indiana Dunes, having summer fun, I was running sprints with my Gary Wirt High School teammate, Jack Sauer. He won our first races by 10 yards, but I kept coming, and before long, I was beating him. That's the way it was done in our family, no matter what the job was—do it right and get it done.

I'D PAY TO PLAY

Playing any game, especially baseball, was more important to me than anything else. I played them all in season at Gary Wirt, winning letters in baseball, football and basketball. Working with my Dad in the iron and steel business also was very satisfying. I had no interest in going to college or opening another textbook. But I knew I could always make a good living as an ironworker. Every day was a different challenge, constructing a wall, changing girders or tearing out old railroad tracks. I'd cut up three-foot sections of track, do a couple arm curls and toss them into a dumpster. It was like getting paid for going to the health club. Whether it was tearing down old buildings or replacing sheet metal, I didn't look on it as a chore. Like hitting a baseball, it was fun.

When I went to a Catholic grade school, I was sort of the class cutup. The nuns would make me clean erasers, and when they found some of my artwork on the wall, like "shithead" written in chalk dust, they knew who to blame. I'd come home with marks on my butt from getting whacked by the canes the nuns used to clean behind the refrigerators.

LET'S MAKE A DEAL

Dad wanted me to go to Andrean, a Catholic high school, but they had a rule against freshmen playing on varsity teams. He drove me back to the school and told the principal "I'll buy the whole team new uniforms if you let my son try out. If he doesn't make it, no problem." He said no, so I ended up going to Gary Wirt. As luck would have it, Andrean was our first opponent the next spring. My first at-bat, I got brushed back by their star pitcher, but the next one he threw, I hit over the stands for a three-run homer. My friends and my Wirt baseball coach, Jerry Troxel, were excited I was coming back to public school. I just wanted to play.

FRIENDS AND FANS

"Ron's the same person he was in school, when nobody thought he'd be a star," said Mike Tebout, a former Gary Wirt High School and Little League teammate of Ron Kittle. "At first, we figured the closest he'd get to the White Sox was sitting in the stands with me and the other guys. Being an ironworker like his dad seemed to be a good way to make a living then. But things went so easy for him in baseball, you could see his confidence growing every year."

And so did Kittle's dream of making it to the top. His Gary Wirt baseball coach, Jerry Troxel, another lifelong friend, enjoys the way his former freshman phenom learned to take success in stride.

"Ron took the time to talk with our players, help out with our baseball clinics and generally encourage young people to raise their sights," Troxel said. "He can do that and still relate to them, because he has the same carefree attitude that made him fun to be around when he was a student. He's the same no-frills Ron Kittle with the White Sox that he was here."

FATHER KNOWS BEST

My Dad bought me my first baseball glove and Converse spikes. I still have that Franklin fielder's glove. I was very proud of wearing my first uniform and walking half a mile in it to the

Miller Girls Softball 1975

Even before signing my first pro contract, I had an interest in teaching and coaching. Members of my 1975 Miller girls softball team included Laura Cooke (top, left), whom I married, and her sisters, Cathy (top, 3rd from left) and Alane (bottom, right).

Little League park. In one of those games, I hit five home runs and just missed a sixth one. Dad still yelled at me after that game, because a friend of mine hit a grounder to me at short-stop and I double-pumped the throw, so he was safe at first. When we got home, Dad said, "Don't ever forget, when the game starts, you have no friends. Throw the sunuvabitch out." I also got no dinner that night, but Mom later slipped me a hot dog.

Baseball was my favorite, right from the start. I picked up a Mickey Mantle model bat when it was bigger than me. Construction workers built a beautiful Senior League ballpark for the older kids across the street from my house, so I used to go in the woods beyond the fence and find baseballs to practice with.

Later, I'd sit in that park with my team, waiting for a pickup game. If we didn't play, I went home mad.

PAIR OF ACES

In high school, two baseball coaches gave my career a big boost. One of them was Jerry Troxel at Gary Wirt. The other was Ken Schreiber, the legendary La Porte coach for 38 years, from 1960 to '98. Ken's teams won seven Indiana state titles and the 1987 national prep championship. Their friendship and advice are as valuable as ever in our frequent get-togethers. Teachers like these two good men help kids want to head in the right direction with their life choices. They certainly did for me.

NO EASY WAY

"Ron Kittle came from the era I appreciated," said Ken Schreiber, La Porte High School's long-time baseball coach. "Ron was making a living at the steel mills, but his

father made sure he got off work to attend a tryout camp in La Porte when I was an area scout for the Dodgers. Players were getting $400 a month in the minors then, and Ron made $750 a week on his job—big money in the 1970s. But he wanted to play baseball, and he had the ability and the guts to get to the top.

"When I started coaching at La Porte, playing ball was considered a privilege by high school kids, and you could discipline them. Then the pros started getting away with steroids, drugs, alcohol and even murder, and it slithered down through the colleges to our kids. They watched on TV and emulated what they saw. The young people still want to excel. It's adult society that tells them to go for the shortcuts, instead of earning their rewards. Now, parents want to sue the teacher, the preacher, everybody who's trying to help their kids learn that the easy way is really the hard way."*

PLAYING TO WIN

Jerry Troxel was an outstanding coach, but Ken Schreiber had a way of blending instruction and discipline that worked. He didn't have better players at La Porte than other schools did. They just played so well together. It's more fun to win that way. One time I saw La Porte win a game on a suicide squeeze bunt, and my dad said, "That's the way to play baseball."

TALENT AND HUNGER

"Ron Kittle was head and shoulders above the other players in high school, but he analyzed everything, looking for ways to improve," said Jerry Troxel, the young slugger's coach at Gary Wirt. "I always thought he had a shot at the majors, so I tried to showcase him for scouts. There were two kids in Northwest Indiana with that kind of

potential—Kittle and Lloyd McClendon from Gary Roosevelt, who played for the Cubs and now is Pittsburgh's manager.

"In 1975, we played in the Plymouth, Indiana, tournament and Ron hit five homers in one day. He had the most powerful swing I'd ever seen, hitting the ball out of sight. Bill Nixon, the Plymouth coach, had Scott Skiles (now the Chicago Bulls coach) and a lot of other hotshots on his team, so he thought they'd run us back to Gary. When Kittle won the MVP award, Bill threw the trophy at him, and it broke. We all laughed about it, but Nixon gave Ron the missing part of the trophy years later, and it's still in Gary Wirt's athletic trophy case."

THE OTHER RON KITTLE

Only Kittle's close friends know this side of the slugger. His media image of a wisecracking slugger worked, so few people saw the other side of this complex, emotional man.

Letting true feelings hang out was not the way it was done in the Kittle family. Slim Kittle taught his six kids to tough it out and face whatever life threw at them. Ron Kittle learned those lessons the hard way. He fought through a long list of injuries to play 10 years in the big leagues.

But there was another side to this hard-driving athlete. Despite the stiff price he paid for success, Kittle found time to listen to other people's concerns and extend a helping hand. His feud with surly superstar Barry Bonds is an example. Even before Kittle's playing career ended, he founded Indiana Sports Charities to supply hope and help for kids in area hospitals.

Ron asks players in all sports to sign balls, caps, jerseys and equipment for auctions at his annual golf outing, with all the money going for kids' care.

Bonds refused to sign, and his confrontation with Kittle is a revealing tale.

BONDS STRIKES OUT

One man in baseball I do not consider a friend is Barry Bonds. In 1993, I bought a couple of his game-worn road jerseys, with San Francisco on the front and his name and number 25 on the back. I paid about $110 of my own money for them, so they could be auctioned off at the golf outing. I did that all the time for stars like Mark McGwire, Sammy Sosa, Derek Jeter and Roger Clemens. When I tell them how their autographs help the cause, every player gladly signs—with one exception.

I walked up to Bonds at his locker in the Wrigley Field visitors' clubhouse, introduced myself and said, "Barry, if you sign these, they'll bring in a lot of money for kids who need help."

Bonds stood up, looked me in the eye and said, "I don't sign for white people." If lightning hits me today, I will swear those were his exact words. Matt Williams and other Giants were in the room and they heard what Bonds said. I stood there for a minute, and the veins in my neck were popping. I've only been that mad a few times in my life. I was going to beat the shit out of him, really kick his ass, but Williams saw what was happening, so he came over and got between us. Matt said, "Ron, that's just the way he is."

I said, "White guys aren't the only ones who get cancer," but Bonds just turned his back on me and walked out of the clubhouse. Somebody must have run in and alerted Dusty Baker, who was the manager of the Giants then. So Dusty came out of his office, put his arm around me, gave me a big old hug and said, "Aw, Kitty, he's just got that shitty attitude again." Dusty gave me an autographed team ball for the auction, but I never got the Bonds jerseys signed. Later, I gave one of them to Scott Paulson, the Wilson sporting goods representative, and shredded the other one. But that day, I drove home from Wrigley Field at about 150 miles an hour and sat there, fuming.

I'll never forget what that man said. So if Barry Bonds is looking for a breath of fresh air to live and I'm the one who has to give it to him, unfortunately, the man will die. I just don't like guys like that.

TIME TO GO PRO

After I graduated from high school, I was working hard every day, building up my strength and still thinking about getting a chance to play ball somewhere. I came home one day, sat on the porch to clean the mud off my boots and just happened to look down. There's this little scrap of paper on the floor, from the Gary *Post-Tribune* sports section. I saw a headline about Los Angeles Dodgers scouts in town for a weekend open tryout. I was planning to work a full shift on Saturday to make double-time pay, $14 an hour. Dad said, "I'll take care of you for those hours," so I went to La Porte for the tryout.

They asked me what position I played and I said, "What do you want me to play?" That same day, John Candelaria of the Pirates pitched a no-hitter against the Dodgers. After they saw me hit some balls over the fence, I heard one of the LA scouts, Glen Van Proyen, say, "I'm glad this kid showed up. There won't be any no-hitters when he's in our lineup." So they offered me $5,000 to sign a contract and I said, "I'll take it." Right away, Dad poked me on the arm. He wanted me to hold out for $10,000, but I would have signed for nothing. I wanted to get going on my dream of being a big-leaguer. When the dream came true, six hard, painful years later, it was right in my back-yard, Chicago, instead of Los Angeles.

PLAYING DODGE(R) BALL

Ken Schreiber, then the La Porte Slicers baseball coach, hosted the tryout that opened the door for Ron Kittle's trip to the big leagues. It wasn't a nonstop limou-

Veteran Dodgers catcher John Roseboro tutors me on the hitting zone.

*sine ride. The Los Angeles Dodgers signed Kittle to his
first pro contract on July 5, 1977, and released him a year
later after deciding that a severe neck injury would end his
career. They were wrong, as the Indiana friends and neigh-*

bors who knew Kittle's determination could have told them.

"A lot of hopeful kids showed up on our field that day," Schreiber recalled. "Only three of them got another look from Dale McReynolds and Glen Van Proyen, the Dodger scouts. When it ended, Dale asked me to set up a pitching machine to watch Kittle and two guys from St. Joseph, Michigan, swing the bat.

"When Ron took his cuts, they said, 'This kid hits the shit out of the ball, but where can we send him to play? It's already midseason for our farm teams.' Ron told me they offered him $5,000 to sign a contract, go home and wait until next spring, but he wanted to get started right away. It had to be one of the all-time bargains, especially if the Dodgers hadn't given up on him so quick."

Fast Disaster

Everybody at the factory where I was an apprentice iron-worker for Local 395, knew I played baseball.

When my dad said, "Don't let this boy get hurt," they looked after me like I was their own son. It was remarkable—they were more scared of him than anything on the job, but they taught me and trained me how to avoid accidents. Looking back, it was kind of funny how safe I was around all those iron fences and molten steel, and yet, I got hurt the first time I played in a pro baseball game.

I signed whatever the Dodgers put in front of me and caught a plane for their gigantic training base in Vero Beach, Florida. No other players were there, so the clubhouse man said, "You must be a rookie."

The place was humongous, like a steel mill behind huge fences. Walking around that whole new world at 4 a.m., with signs reading Koufax Lane and Drysdale Lane, I was in awe. But it wasn't until the next spring that the Dodgers sent me to

Clinton, Iowa, in the Midwest League. I wound up eating Easter dinner alone at Kentucky Fried Chicken, squeezing into the last seat open in the place. When I tell that story, everybody remembers their first holiday away from home, missing Mom's cooking and the family at the table.

I don't remember many details of that first game and the collision at the plate that almost made me an ex-player, or even worse, an invalid. All I knew then was that my right arm was numb and I couldn't take a full swing at bat. It was a broken neck, but I tried to keep playing at Clinton and Lethbridge, Ontario, until the pain got so bad, I had to start seeing doctors. The Dodgers paid the bills for neck surgery in 1978, but they figured I was through, so they cut me loose. The word was out that I couldn't play anymore.

2

MINOR LEAGUES, MAJOR DREAMS
From a Broken Neck to 90 Homers in Two Seasons

NO GATOR AID

I wasn't exactly a barrel of laughs after finding out that I broke my neck in that first pro game. I never feared anything, except the uncertainty and the dread of thinking that my body wouldn't let me do what my mind knew I could on a baseball field. It didn't help when doctors examined me, frowned at my neck X-rays and predicted that anything more athletic than crossing the street was out of the question for me. All Dad and I cared about was getting me back into playing shape. I had a broken neck, but he insisted it was nothing more than a sore arm.

So I went to 1978 spring training with the Dodgers, played the outfield and did what sandlot players do. When somebody hit a homer, I climbed over the low fence to retrieve the baseball. A coach trotted out and said, "Hey, kid, we don't go after balls beyond that fence. It's a swamp, with lots of alligators looking for their lunch."

Four young Dodgers hopefuls at our Florida spring training base in 1978 (left to right): Dan Henry, me, Tim Roche and Mike Scioscia. Only Scioscia and I made it to the majors.

Ending up as a gator's entrée was about the only bad thing that didn't happen to me that spring. I had little mobility, my neck hurt and all of a sudden, there was no roster spot for me. Jim Lefebvre, later the Cubs manager, was in the LA organization then, and he encouraged me to go rehab at Dodger Stadium.

But I got released soon after, at the lowest point of my life, loaded with mental and physical pain. I didn't want to talk to anyone, so I went home and got a job with American Bridge Co., pulling metal sheets 200 feet by rope. In two months, I was all muscle again. And baseball was still on my mind.

AHEPA GOOD NEWS

Thankfully, a man named Dean Stravakas called me up and said, "Come and play summer ball for the AHEPA team I manage. It's a Greek team without any Greek players on it." AHEPA? It stands for American Hellenic Educational and Progressive Assn., but for me, it's spelled G-O-D-S-E-N-D. One game with them, I came up with a Bill Madlock M110 black bat and hit the longest homer I remember.

The bat broke, but the ball must have traveled 500 feet onto the I-294 expressway. One immediate reaction I heard was that Roland Hemond and Billy Pierce, the great little White Sox lefty, were driving by, saw the ball bouncing on the road and arranged a Comiskey Park tryout for me. More likely, it happened because a businessman and baseball fan named Cecil Messer, who had dealings with Pierce's envelope company in Chicago, told him about me. I like the monster homer version more, but however it happened, I'll always be grateful to Stravakas, who told me, "Ron, your story is better than that Rudy guy at Notre Dame. He only played a few seconds, but look what you did with the White Sox."

BILLY THE (GOOD) KID

Billy Pierce, one of the classiest, as well as one of the best, pitchers ever to wear a White Sox uniform, is still a Chicago civic asset, long after he retired from baseball. The stylish southpaw won 186 games for them, then stuck around to run a successful business and get involved in many charitable and youth programs. Pierce now serves on the board of directors for Ron Kittle's Indiana Sports Charities. He's a close friend of long-time Sox front-office icon Roland Hemond.

"Cecil Messer called in 1978 to tell me about this kid named Kittle," Pierce said. "He had been signed by the Dodgers and got a lot of bad breaks, but Cecil thought I should see the way he was hitting homers on the AHEPA team my son (Bill Jr.) used to play for. I had lunch with Ron and I was impressed by his sincerity. He didn't strike me as a hot dog at all."

So Pierce telephoned Hemond. Kittle was topic A of that conversation.

"Billy knew I was aware he would check out a player before recommending him to the White Sox," Hemond said. "He loves this team and he'll help us any way he can. He sure did when he said 'Roland, there's a kid playing ball out here in the Chicago suburbs I think you should take a gander at.' AHEPA's season was over, so I arranged for Kittle to come to Comiskey Park and let our people look him over."

THE COMEBACK KID

I went right from work to the ballpark, dirty, sweaty and tired, when the White Sox told me about the tryout on September 4, just two months after the Dodgers wrote me off. They gave me uniform pants and a beat-up Sox hat. Iron flecks were caked on the only pair of glasses I had. After a few throws in the outfield, I said "I'm loose," grabbed a Bill Naharodny bat, and they put veteran right-hander Bruce Dal Canton on the mound to see what I could do with big-league pitching. His first one was right down the middle. I swung and missed it by 10 feet. The White Sox reserves, waiting their turn to hit, could have said, "Get this big lug outa here," but I guess they had been in my spot before. So they stood quietly around the batting cage while I dribbled the next few pitches on the ground.

I stepped out for a minute, took a deep breath, came back in and hit the next one into the upper deck in left field. All of a sudden, people were crowding around the cage, including George Brett and some other Royals, to watch me put on a show. I hit about eight or ten more into the stands, and one of them sailed out of the park through one of the big windows behind the stands. Somebody said, 'Holy shit, this kid can hit.' When I was through, Naharodny shook my hand and said, "If they offer you less than $1 million, don't sign." It was about $999,000 less than that, but I still think the Man Upstairs was looking after me.

On my last swing, the lens fell out of my glasses. If that had happened a dozen pitches earlier, I might still be climbing those iron and steel girders for a living.

RON FILLS THE BILL

Roland Hemond got tied up with paperwork in his office during Ron Kittle's tryout. It was just after the roster limits ended, so the general manager was figuring out ways to beef up the White Sox for the 1980s. He soon found out that help already was on the way, in the thunder of Kittle's booming bat.

"Bill Veeck liked to sit in the dugout and watch those tryouts," Hemond said. "He was impressed by Ron's strong throwing arm, but when he came up to bat and baseballs began flying into the stands, it was clear that we had stumbled onto something.

"Charlie Evranian, our farm director, called and said, 'Hey, this kid Kittle is really hitting some bombs. Bill Veeck's down there and he doesn't want to let him get out of the ballpark.' I knew what Veeck meant: Sign Kittle, pronto. As I recall, he came into my office with his Dad and signed a minor-league contract. I don't recall, so he'd have to tell you whether he got $500 or $1,000 up front. Whatever the amount, it was a pretty good investment for the White Sox."

NO LOOKING BACK

They wanted me to meet Bill Veeck right after the tryout, but I was hyperventilating. So I helped Glen Rosenbaum (Sox traveling secretary and batting practice pitcher), another good guy from Northwest Indiana, pick up the baseballs on the field, sat in the stands with my Dad for a few innings, fell asleep and had him drive me home. I must have slept 12 or 14 hours straight, but when I woke up, I knew I'd be wearing a White Sox uniform before long. My dream was alive and kicking again, so it was up to me to make it happen.

The road back to Chicago led me through Appleton, Wisconsin; Knoxville, Tennessee; Glens Falls, New York; and finally to Edmonton, Alberta. It was a tough trip, but I had fun, met some wonderful people, like my good buddy Greg Walker, dealt with still more injuries and weathered a few disappointments. If I could, I'd do it all over again in a heartbeat, although this time a lot more pain-free.

It didn't take long for me to find out what a ferocious competitor Tony La Russa was. He was managing at Des Moines, Iowa, in the spring of 1979, and I stayed with the White Sox to play his team an exhibition. Wayne Nordhagen split his thumb on a foul tip, so I volunteered to catch. I heard Tony say, "Don't worry, we're not gonna run on you," so I knew I'd better be ready for anything. Sure enough, they tried to steal right away with runners on first and third. I threw out Bobby Molinaro at second base, took the throw home and buried the guy sliding in. Double play. I flipped the ball to Tony and said, "You can run on me any time." He wants to win, no matter what, and he knows I do, too.

Before settling in left field when I got to Chicago, I played several positions in the minor leagues. I even saw action behind the plate at Appleton, Wisconsin, in 1980.

SWAT, MEET SWEET

There were good times in the minor leagues. I made a lot of friends with players, especially my good buddy Greg Walker, who's now doing a outstanding job as the White Sox hitting instructor.

Besides passing along a lot of the fundamentals we both learned from Charley Lau, I'm sure Greg shows them how Swat (me) and Sweet (him) used to do it when we were teammates in a couple of minor leagues and later in Chicago.

The trophies I got for being named Most Valuable Player in the Pacific Coast League (1982) and the Eastern League (1981), along with the '82 Minor League Player of the Year Award mean as much to me as the AL Rookie of the Year honor that came a year later. They remind me that I made the long climb back

I'm taking a swing during the 1982 season in Edmonton. That was the one season that I stayed healthy from start to finish, and my numbers reflected that—50 homers, 144 RBIs and a .345 batting average.

after being told my baseball career was over almost before it started. The places I played in and the people I met in all of them, on and off the field, made things a lot more interesting. Some of the teams I played for have disbanded or gone to some other city, but the memories remain. That's why I felt sad when a friend told me Canadian press sources were running hail-and-farewell stories about the demise of the Edmonton Trappers, the class AAA team I played for in 1982.

That season started off on a down note for me, at the end of spring training with the White Sox. Tony La Russa called me into his office to say I was being farmed out to Edmonton, adding, "If you do well, we can bring you back." That was very disappointing news, because I knew then I could hit big-league pitching. When the call finally came, it was at the tail end of the AL schedule, but I didn't spend any time feeling sorry for myself. Instead, I staged the kind of 1982 dream season as an individual in Edmonton that the 1983 White Sox enjoyed as a team in Chicago. I tore into Pacific Coast League pitching for 50 home runs, 144 RBIs and a .345 average. Fans in that sports-happy town awarded me the sort of celebrity status usually reserved for Wayne Gretzky, their hockey superstar, and I spent some enjoyable times palling around with the Great One.

KITTLE'S 50 NIFTIEST

Baseball fans in Edmonton were left only with memo-ries when the Trappers, their team in the class AAA Pacific Coast League, ended a 24-year run in the Canadian province of Alberta.

First on the list of magic moments for Trappers fans was Ron Kittle's 50th home run in 1982. In his last at-bat of that season, the bespectacled slugger slammed No. 50 over the fence at old Renfrew Park. It set a PCL single-season home run record that still stands. A new Northern

League franchise will come to Edmonton in 2005, but things won't be the same.

"Kittle was on fire all through that season," said Al Coates, the long-time Trappers broadcaster. "He struck like lightning."

Chuck Moser, an Edmonton fan, still recalls the trajectory of Kittle's blasts. "When Ron hit them, they took off like rockets," Moser said. "Watching them disappear into the night sky was awesome."

NOLAN'S 1-HITTER (ME)

Getting the word that Nolan Ryan had purchased the Edmonton Trappers and would move them from Canada to Texas brought a reminiscent chuckle to Ron Kittle. Ferocious competitor Ryan pitched seven no-hit games in his magnificent career, but the fireballing right-hander didn't hesitate to hit a batter when it served his purpose.

"I homered off Nolan, and the next time up, he hit me on purpose," Kittle said. "When he was with the Rangers, I broke up a Comiskey Park no-hitter he was working on with a little squib single. He threw that heat right at my knuckles, and I almost broke my hand swinging at it. Rafael Palmiero, the first baseman, tripped on his shoelaces, so I got the only hit for the White Sox. I'm standing on the bag, holding my sore thumb, and Ryan climbed back on the mound, turned around and stared right though me. I knew what he was thinking: 'You SOB, how lucky can you get?' Raffy was cracking up, trying not to laugh out loud. I just took a healthy cut, and that's what happens in baseball.

"Next time we faced them in Texas, Ryan went right after me. His 95-mph fastball left a welt on my bicep. So I picked up the ball, pretended to take a bite like it was an apple and tossed it back to him. When I got to first base, Palmiero asked 'Did it hurt?' It sure did, but I wasn't going to let Ryan know that."

A GREAT (ONE) GESTURE

I was healthy enough to play a full season at Edmonton, and I made the most of it—50 homers, 144 ribbies and a .345 average. It was a kick when Wayne Gretzky, another pretty good player from Edmonton, came to Comiskey Park on May 2, 1983, to give me the minor league Player of the Year Award for '82. "Ron was kind of a hero up there," the Great One said. "Fans got excited when he hit the ball out of sight, and so did I."

THE HEAT'S ON

The pressure to perform was waiting for me as soon as I got to Chicago, because Sox fans were hungry for a winner. They chanted for me when I was still at Edmonton, every time one of my homers in Triple-A got posted on the Comiskey Park scoreboard. This story about my call up to the White Sox appeared in the *Chicago Tribune* on August 31, 1982, a few days before my major-league debut:

Memo to Ron Kittle: Hurry, kid!

Kittle's booming bat is on its way, at last, to Comiskey Park. Even if the slugging outfielder is the reincarnation of Babe Ruth, it's too late for the White Sox, at least in 1982. Kittle and three other players have been recalled in a last-ditch search for a miracle. But Kittle is the Sox' hope for the future, although the present's beyond redemption. Manager Tony La Russa indicated the newcomer would debut Friday against Texas.

"We want to see what Kittle can do," La Russa said. "There's great interest about this kid in Chicago."

That story, by a sportswriter named Bob Logan, told me the expectations were pretty high. I soon found out that was true, although my own expectations were even higher. What I had to prove to anybody else wasn't as important to me as what I had to prove to myself. I had been preparing almost all my life for this moment. No matter how high the bar was set, it was up to me to clear that hurdle. So I didn't mind when White Sox players were ready with the needle when I walked into the clubhouse to pick out some lumber and head for the batting cage. "Hey, the new Babe Ruth is here," said pitcher Rich Dotson, my former Knoxville teammate. And lefty Steve Trout, soon to get traded to the Cubs, added, "We'll have to put some guys with gloves on the left-field roof."

If anybody had predicted that almost exactly a year after Trout's kidding remark, I really would bounce two home runs over that roof, would I have believed them? Maybe. But I always felt it was better to do something before you talk about doing it. When I made the club the next spring, I wanted to lighten the atmosphere with a wisecrack or two, especially since nobody else on the White Sox was doing too much talking. Harold Baines, the original quiet man, told me he felt comfortable on the White Sox because Tony La Russa encouraged us to play ball and not worry about the media. It's true that Tony was always willing to take the blame when things didn't work out, instead of laying it on his players. He got our respect for doing that, but I didn't accept losing a game as a legitimate excuse for hiding in the trainer's room until the writers left the clubhouse.

I never thought I was a superstar, and I didn't try to act like one. When I saw a kid in a wheelchair behind a crowd of autograph hunters, I made it a point to speak to him, without looking around to see if a photographer was there. If the people at the ballpark had fun, I enjoyed it along with them. I tried to be sociable to the umpires, too, because they have a tough job.

LaPOINTLESS TASK

Ron Kittle learned in the minor leagues, from pitchers like Dave LaPoint, that changing speeds ruins a hitter's timing. LaPoint, a junk-balling lefty, now owns a bar in Glens Falls, N.Y., the town where Kittle flailed in vain at his dipsy-doo deliveries.

"I went back to Glens Falls and stopped in Dave's place to say hello," Kittle related. "He has a nonstop video above the bar, rerunning his strikeouts of Mark McGwire, Jose Canseco, Don Baylor and me on a dinky change or a curve in the dirt. All of us right-handed power hitters had the same weakness. I asked him where were the shots of guys hitting one of his pitches out of sight. He said, "Kitty, I must have lost those tapes."

I made several great friends on my way up to the majors. Here I hold court with a group of youngsters in Glens Falls, New York.

A Guessing Game

I was a guess hitter, and sometimes it was absolutely impossible to lay off that slow stuff. You always have to be ready for the fastball, but so many pitchers have hard sliders that can make you look bad.

For anyone trying to make a living by getting two and a half hits in every 10 cuts at big-league pitching, it's a confidence game, an emotional roller-coaster that you ride from April to October. That's why it helps so much to have a morale booster like Chicken Willie Thompson, the White Sox clubhouse man, around to pick you up when you're down. Willie is larger than life, and he speaks the ballplayers' language. I wore No. 21 at Edmonton, but first thing when I went to spring training with the Sox, Willie handed me a jersey with No. 42 on the back. He said, "Kitty, you work as hard as Jackie Robinson did, so here's his number. Besides, you can be twice as good as you were with that No. 21."

50, Count 'em, 50

Actually, I should have made it with the White Sox on 1982. I showed them in spring training that I could hit big-league pitching, but they had brought in Steve Kemp, paying him $600,000 to hit 19 homers. So I went to Edmonton and hit 50 that season, along with 144 RBIs, for $2,500 a month.

What I said then, and I still say now is true—the dollars didn't matter to me. I knew I could always go back to climbing up those steel girders in Gary and make a decent living. I just wanted a chance to prove I belonged in the majors. The way my neck, back, shoulders and the rest of me kept hurting, I figured it better not take too long.

But when you hit 90 home runs over two seasons—40 in 1981 at Glens Falls, New York, and then 50 in the Triple-A Pacific Coast League, somebody has to pay attention. I knew I'd have to prove myself defensively, too, but after making all the plays as a shortstop and a catcher for years, doing the job in the outfield wasn't that hard. And it helped to hear that White Sox fans were rooting for me even before I got called up.

Whenever I hit a homer for Edmonton, they put it up on the Comiskey Park scoreboard and the fans yelled, "Bring up Kittle!" Except for some bone chips in my right thumb, 1982 was the most pain-free season I ever had, so I made the most of it.

So when the 25-man roster limit ended on September 1, I got the opportunity of my lifetime. One day later, I was sitting in the Comiskey Park dugout wearing a White Sox uniform, still numb after the long flight from Edmonton. Tony La Russa sent me up to pinch hit, and I still remember the small crowd making a lot of noise when I stepped in to face Jeff Zahn of the Texas Rangers. I fouled off a couple of pitches and he struck me out on a changeup that was nothing like the stuff I'd been seeing in the PCL.

I went back and sat down, expecting nothing but dead silence. Instead, the veterans told me it was a good at-bat. It's those little things that stick in your mind years later.

DOUBLE OR NOTHING?

On September 4, 1982, I almost got sandbagged by the umpire, Ken Kaiser, into turning my first hit into an out. I doubled down the left-field line and Kenny came up to me and said, real low, "Foul ball."

When I stepped off the bag, he grabbed me and said, "Stay there, you got a hit. I was just kidding." I was mad and excited at the same time, but I still have the ball I hit off Frank Tanana, a tough pitcher.

One thing hitters never forget is their first home run in the big time. I got that off Frank Viola of the Twins on October 2. I saw the ball on the ground in the outfield and I thought, "Did it hit a speaker and bounce back?" Then I saw the home run signal, and my feet didn't touch the ground all the way around the bases. When the reporters came in after the game, I told them I'd hit a few more if I played in that Minnesota wind tunnel. What I really thought to myself was, "This is the start of what I always wanted."

An Honest Count

Ron Kittle's quirky sense of humor fit right in with his new White Sox teammates. Tom Paciorek demonstrated that to the delighted rookie one late-season afternoon in Oakland, when both clubs were quietly closing out the 1982 schedule. A few hundred customers showed up, so Paciorek decided to take his own combined census and head count. From the Sox dugout, he was within shouting distance of all the fans, who sat in front-row box seats.

"Hey, what's your name?" Wimpy asked them in turn, writing each one down, including the beer vendors. They joined the "crowd," plunking down their cases and proclaiming, "If you want a beer, come and get it." Paciorek's list eventually grew to 238 names, Kittle recalled, but his plan to ship the document to Cooperstown fizzled, for lack of postage.

3

THIS ROOK'S WORTH A LOOK

A New South Side Slugger

ONE-TWO PUNCH

I came to spring training in 1983 with the feeling that I belonged in the majors. The White Sox were the right bunch of guys I wanted to be with, and Chicago was the place where I wanted to play. My buddy, Greg Walker, came up with me, both of us hoping to continue the success we had together in the minors. I first met Greg in spring training 1979, but I was the bullpen catcher, because the White Sox were letting a kid from Boston College do all the catching. So the first question Greg asked me was, "Are you ever going to play?"

It turned out we played together a lot, made the 1980 All-Star team in Class A at Appleton, Wisconsin, and kicked the stuffing out of a Triple-A team with Dave Stewart and other guys who made the majors.

Walker and I hit so well next to each other in the lineup, the writers started calling us "Swat and Sweet."

Greg Walker and I, labeled "Swat and Sweet" for the way we bashed baseballs together in the minor leagues, were ready to do the same for the White Sox when we arrived at Comiskey Park in 1983.

He was Sweet for that smooth swing, and I was Swat because the fans enjoyed watching me put on a power show in batting practice. We got along right away, roomed together for three years in the minors and had to fight through some tough luck to get a chance with the White Sox. Walker was hitting over .400 for Edmonton in 1982 when he broke his wrist and was out three months.

Besides hitting well back-to-back, Walker and I made a pretty good team in the knife and fork league, too. Somebody asked what we did best, and I told the truth: "Eat." We still like to do that when we get together. To tell the truth, we don't need fancy restaurants or exotic food. Greg and I are not connoisseurs— we're consumers.

But for a Southern guy—Greg's originally from Georgia— and an ironworker's kid from Gary, Indiana, we got along and helped each other to get where we wanted to go. We made good roommates, even though Greg read every sports page and box score he could find and I was up and out early in the morning. When Greg and Carmen had a daughter, Kaycee, I was her designated baby sitter.

MAJOR AND MINOR PALS

"Ron and I would have been friends wherever we met, in or out of baseball," said Greg Walker, who became hitting coach for the White Sox in 2004. "We rode those minor-league buses for thousands of miles, picked each other up and got to the majors together. Kitty always manages to remind me that I made two errors when the White Sox lost the 1983 season opener in Texas. I think he's still mad because I played first base in that game, and he didn't get into the lineup until the next night.

"I can't forget the suspense in spring training, when we battled to stay with the club. Kittle was confident he'd make it, but I wasn't so sure. We kept reading in Chicago

papers about me or him getting traded. I was on edge until Tony La Russa told me, 'You're not going anywhere.' That enabled me to become Kitty's traveling secretary in 1983, fielding the phone calls from everybody who wanted to put his outrageous opinions on the air or in print."

A BOUQUET FROM ROSE

Spring training, 1983, was no bed of roses for Ron Kittle and Greg Walker, a couple of rookies who were looked on as longshots to stick with the White Sox. Daily speculation in sportswriters' stories from the Sarasota, Florida, training base pointed to Kittle's alleged fielding deficiencies and whether roster room could be found to carry Walker as a spare first baseman and pinch hitter. Sox Manager Tony La Russa, always ready with a candid comment on his team's prospects, sounded skeptical about both newcomers at the outset. Despite some mammoth Kittle clouts in exhibition games, the jury was out, at least until Pete Rose got a look at him.

Rose was with the Phillies then, chasing Ty Cobb's all-time record of 4,191 hits. Though he specialized in singles, Charlie Hustle could spot a power hitter a mile away. His eyes lit up when he saw Kittle slam pitches over the palm trees and out of Payne Park in batting practice. Picking his spot, Rose waited until La Russa and Kittle huddled behind the batting cage, sauntered up to the Sox manager and said, "Tony, there's no way I would keep this kid out of the lineup every day." Then he winked at Kittle and walked away.

HORNING IN ON JIMMY

When Jimmy Piersall dismissed catcher Carlton Fisk as "over the hill" on his postgame radio show early in 1983, the White

Sox severed ties with the colorful, controversial analyst. Piersall had lost his job as Harry Caray's livewire TV partner two years earlier, after his famous "horny broads" remark about some baseball wives.

Caray, feeding on Sox fans' ire about the move, told owners Jerry Reinsdorf and Eddie Einhorn, "You guys became villains by taking Jimmy out of the broadcast booth. Why not repair the damage by putting us back together on the TV team?"

Reinsdorf quickly swung back at that pitch. "Harry, I'll be up in heaven looking down before Piersall broadcasts another one of our games," he said.

THREE-RING CIRCUS A HIT SHOW

I don't believe the players paid as much attention to Caray and Piersall as people in the front office did.

We were too busy trying to get our act together. I could tell before we left Florida at the end of spring training that the White Sox would be contenders. There was too much talent all over this 1983 roster to discount us, so we didn't worry about what the media thought or who was feuding with whom off the field. Along with proven players and rookies ready to contribute, like Greg Walker and me, we had the right blend of personalities. You don't find that too often. Even most winners have some guys unwilling to give themselves up for the team, but as long as things go well, dissent gets swept under the rug. Nobody on the Sox started pointing fingers when we didn't get out of the gate fast enough.

Early in the season, after another tough loss, I recall Tony La Russa saying, "Other than a good attitude, we don't have much going for us right now." What we did have was a good mix of people with a sense of humor. You couldn't sit around and brood in our clubhouse. Not in the same room or even the same town with Marc "Booter" Hill, Dennis Lamp, Jerry Koosman,

Kevin Hickey and Art Kusnyer, the bullpen coach with a load of raunchy, funny stories. And maybe the loosest character of all was Willie "Chicken Man" Thompson. He ran the White Sox clubhouse breezily as the equipment manager, resident philosopher, joke-teller, all-around good guy and the only man I ever saw who could swallow a whole chicken leg, bones and all.

STAY LOOSE, GUYS

Some fans still cling to Tony La Russa's image as a grim-jawed managerial taskmaster, despite the success he's had in both the American and National Leagues. The White Sox found out early in 1983 that he knew how to loosen up and when to crack the whip. After getting swept in the season-opening series and playing sloppy baseball in those three defeats by the Texas Rangers, the players didn't know what to expect from him. Instead of a dressing down, they got salad dressing and all the trimmings at a team party.

"After starting out with three straight losses, some fans think I should kick my players and lock them in their rooms," La Russa said. "Anyone who believes that doesn't know how important it is for pro athletes to relax."

So the players and coaches partied hearty at a belated bachelor party for reliever Kevin Hickey, who married Terri Witt just before the Sox broke training camp in Florida. It went on until the wee hours.

"Look at these guys," La Russa said when his bedraggled squad tottered in for a noon workout. "They're still groggy." It was a demonstration of the managerial skill that pulled the Sox together and later paid off for winning teams in Oakland and St. Louis. The Sox flew to Detroit and eased their collective hangover by pounding the Tigers twice, with Ron Kittle's three-run homer the difference in the second victory.

"Chicago fans kind of expect me to do that," Kittle told reporters of the early signs that he'd live up to their high expectations.

ALL OVER THE AL

Seeing the big, beautiful American League ballparks and adjusting to the different conditions in each of them added spice to my first turn around the league. Certainly, walking into Yankee Stadium for the first time has to be an emotional experience for any player or fan not made of stone. That was the way it was for me. Looking around at the stage where Babe Ruth, Joe DiMaggio, Mickey Mantle and other great players took the spotlight has to speed up your pulse.

Boston has the same kind of tradition. History is everywhere you look there, including Fenway Park, with that imposing Green Monster, a beckoning target in left field that serves as sort of a wailing wall for those fanatical Red Sox fans. I tried to turn it into a whaling wall by lofting a few home runs over its 37-foot height. When rain wiped out batting practice on May 30, before my first game at Fenway, I was disappointed. It turned out to be a break. If I'd tried to uppercut some balls over the Monster in BP, I might have tried it during the game. Instead, I kept my level swing against left-hander Bruce Hurst and lined a two-run homer in the fourth inning.

JUST THE FACTS, MAN

Early in the '83 season, Tony told me he had a gut feeling about what to do in a certain situation. I said, "Skip, it's probably just your ulcer flaring up." He worried about what to do on every pitch, but that was his managerial style. The White Sox organization started looking at things his way, too. Instead of just throwing a pitcher or a hitter into a certain spot, they would check out the statistical probabilities first.

That's when the computer era was first taking hold, and it soon spread throughout every level of pro sports. Of course, when you're managing a team with Carlton Fisk, Greg Luzinski

Tony La Russa worried about what to do on every pitch and introduced computer analysis to the White Sox clubhouse. In the end, this was exactly what we needed.

and Harold Baines on the roster, you have to start the main guys every day. There's really only a limited number of times when you alternate players, if somebody hits better against a righty or a lefty. Tony always showed up well-armed with stats, figures and charts on who did what against who in every ballpark.

PUDGE WON'T BUDGE

When we got bogged down early, all you saw in the papers was the feud between Carlton Fisk and Tony La Russa. Pudge Fisk wasn't hitting the way he could, and he was unhappy because his pitchers weren't pitching the way they should have been.

Old-time Sox fans weren't crazy about Tony's button-down image and his reliance on computer statistics. Whenever he came out of the dugout, they booed him.

The ones I knew kept talking about the good old days with Al Lopez and Eddie Stanky and Paul Richards and Jimmy Dykes. I know they were good managers, but so was Tony. There still was a lot of pressure on the owners to fire him, and if things hadn't turned around at the All-Star break, it might have happened. All I can say is, thank God it didn't.

A NUDGE FOR PUDGE

The bad blood between White Sox manager Tony La Russa and his catcher, Carlton Fisk, came close to real bloodshed during their nose-to-nose confrontation between games of a July 12 doubleheader in Oakland. Fisk, batting a puny .136, felt he was an unfair target of criticism because the Sox pitching staff was nibbling at the plate instead of attacking the hitters. Understandably, from La Russa's vantage point, the veteran receiver was not taking charge at the plate, or behind it.

"It was almost like 1984," said the literate Fisk, referring not to the next season, but to George Orwell's epic novel. "Big Brother was watching me. Trying to help our pitchers affected my hitting and my approach to the game. Suddenly, somebody's showing me computer printouts to let people know what hand they should wipe their nose with."

As always, La Russa refused to back down. He gambled that having it out with Fisk, a proud, stubborn New Englander, would either make or break the struggling Sox.

The way the catcher and the team reacted proved their manager was right.

"When I went to Pudge with problems, they hadn't been dreamed up by me," La Russa said. "After we talked, he found a solution for them and became the Hall of Fame catcher we needed."

STEADY AS HE GOES

A major reason why the good ship S.S. Soxcess sailed safely through some stormy seas was Roland Hemond's stabilizing influence. Jerry Reinsdorf, the White Sox chairman, admitted he was close to pulling the plug on manager Tony La Russa when the team floundered into June.

"Roland always has the biggest voice in anything, especially player decisions," Reinsdorf said.

That included the tough choice to bring in Bobby Winkles, Sox player development chief, for a thumbs-up-or-down analysis of La Russa's grip on the struggling Sox. With advice from Hemond that patience would validate Tony's ability, Winkles made a favorable report, the axe didn't descend on La Russa and the Sox soon caught fire. Hemond knew it all along, though he seldom said, "I told you so."

THE CHOICE WAS RIGHT

Hemond had to make some hard choices on players right in the middle of the 1983 season. The fans and media were yelling for him to bring in an established closer, like Seattle's Bill Caudill or Ron Davis of the Twins.

When the White Sox started winning consistently in June, the uproar grew louder. We couldn't get over the hump, some armchair relievers insisted, without that extra added ingredient. But Roland turned down a straight swap of Rich Dotson, our No. 2 starter, for Caudill, which would have been disastrous. Dotson ended up winning 22 games that season, while the bullpen resembled a resort because Sox relievers needed relief from boredom in the closing months.

Instead, Hemond switched second basemen with the Mariners, getting Julio Cruz for Tony Bernazard. It was a steal, with Juice Cruz and Rudy Law combining to burn up the basepaths for us. Even the skeptics had to admit Hemond was a big winner there. With Roland in our corner, I always figured the Sox were, too.

NO. 1 MOVE IS TO NO. 2

The whole complexion of the team changed when Tony moved Fisk into the No. 2 slot in the batting order. Our leadoff man, Rudy Law, kept stealing bases, so Pudge got a lot of fastballs to hit.

Rudy drove the pitchers crazy whenever he got on, and that helped Fisk to relax and start tattooing the ball. In the second half of the season, Pudge came out of his shell and opened up to the media.

The fans had always been in his corner, so they ate it up. He deserved all the credit he got for taking charge of the pitchers, even though they did things the way Tony and his pitching coach, Dave Duncan, wanted them to.

THE TRUTH HURTS

Bruce Levine, the "Baseball Insider" for ESPN radio in Chicago, has a pretty good memory of the 1983 season.

"Ron Kittle's one of the most honest people in baseball," Levine said. "He was so honest, it probably cost him a few years off his career. He wouldn't alibi to the manager or the media when he was horseshit. He'd come right out and tell us, 'I was horseshit today.'"

"In the sports pages, his quote would read, 'I was horsebleep.' One of the most refreshing players I ever met. A good guy and an unforgettable Chicago sports character. He'd make fun of the clichés everybody else used to alibi about going zero for four."

NO BELL PRIZE

Greg Walker and I both started off hitting well in 1983 spring training. For a couple of guys not even expected to be around on Opening Day, we were doing all right. Still, all spring I kept hearing the White Sox were looking to put me in a trade package that would solve their third-base problem by luring Buddy Bell from Texas or Lance Parrish from Detroit.

As my friend and mentor, Roland Hemond, the astute Sox general manager, kept telling me, the best move sometimes turns out to be none at all. With the Swat and Sweet Boys—that's Walker and Kittle, for those of you keeping score at home—contributing and the way Vance Law proved he could be our everyday third baseman, Roland was proved right once again.

Roland Gets 'Em Rolling

Roland Hemond's blend of experience, judgment and ability to keep calm while the boat was rocking played a major role in helping La Russa get through those tough times in April and May. Sox fans kept calling for the manager's head on a platter, and signs of frustration began creeping into the clubhouse. Veteran Tom Paciorek, riled by his part-time status, let loose a blast at the manager that he soon regretted.

If the White Sox don't want a .300 hitter, someone else will," Paciorek lamented. "This club ain't exactly the 1927 Yankees. I want out."

Naturally, the anti-La Russa wolfpack pounced when they read Wimpy's wail, interpreting it as a sign that the Sox skipper was losing control of a sinking ship. What was needed at that moment was a steady hand on the tiller. Nobody in baseball was better than Hemond at restoring perspective to such emotional situations.

The battle-tested GM wasted no time proving once again why his calm tone is one of the game's most respected voices. For eager rookies like me, as well as the struggling Sox veterans, it was just what we needed to hear.

"If the fans and media are patient with Tony, this team will produce for him," Hemond predicted. "It's not easy to avoid pointing fingers when things go bad, but that's what it takes to build a winner."

Panic Strikes Out

It takes a winner to know one. Just as genial Roland foresaw, the White Sox got rolling. The improvement was gradual but steady while tempers cooled, frazzled nerves unwound and batting eyes refocused. Before the Terminate Tony crowd could paint fresh signs or think up new jeers, the Sox relocated from outhouse to penthouse in the AL West.

We hit the pits on May 26, when Floyd Bannister lost a 3-1 toughie to Texas before a hostile Comiskey Park crowd, falling eight games under .500 at 16-24.

I didn't think about it at the time, but my two-run homer the next night off Frank Tanana actually was the starting point for Sox resurgence. That made the difference in LaMarr Hoyt's 3-2 win over the Rangers. To tell the truth, I was fooled on a low outside pitch from Tanana, so I sort of one-handed my swing. The ball took off like a rocket, slamming into the upper-deck facade in left field.

GOTTA HAND IT TO HIM

Some American League pitchers could claim they were throwing at Ron Kittle in self-defense after he started launching unguided missiles in 1983. The sheer strength of the White Sox rookie was awesome to the fans and frightening to the flingers who had to face him from a mere 60 feet, six inches away.

Kittle's first home run of the season, on April 8, soared into Tiger Stadium's left-field upper deck. His victim, Detroit ace Jack Morris, stood on the mound in disbelief, watching the drive vanish.

"Kittle's either the strongest man in the world or else he's using a corked bat," Morris said after taking the rap in a 7-5 Sox victory. "He one-handed that ball into the upper deck. The pitch wasn't even over the plate."

GO-GO WHITE SOX-CESS

I was not going for a home run whenever I came to bat. It felt good to hit 35 and set a record for White Sox rookies, but you can't look for the fastball all the time.

Changeups were murder for guys like me, who let it all hang out with each swing. You see the same windup, motion and arm action, and then the pitch sinks when you commit. Spotting the rotation on curves and sliders was easier. My biggest fault was trying to hit every pitch, instead of hanging back a bit and learning to relax. I'm never like that, no matter what I do. For me, it's full speed ahead, all the time. The Go-Go White Sox came before me, but I was one of them, mentally at least.

A GENTLE GIANT

With my size and strength, it's a good thing I didn't try to take my frustrations out on other people, especially pitchers who threw at me. When I came on the scene, hitting a bunch of home runs, the word got around pretty quick.

I was getting brushed back almost nightly, and Tony La Russa was not the kind of manager to let opponents get away with that stuff. He always stood up for his players and he was the first one out of the dugout when things started to get ugly.

Tony was especially protective of Harold Baines, because he was skin and bones, so getting hit anywhere could have hurt him. The rest of us had some beef and blubber to absorb the blows.

HOLD THOSE TIGER FANS

On occasion, the fans can get temperamental, too. The nicest thing they called the White Sox in Milwaukee was "Ugly," and they were talking about our faces, not our winning ways. Bad as those Brewer backers got, the ugliest scene I saw happened one sunny afternoon in Detroit, with old Tiger Stadium packed to the rafters. It was downright scary.

I was in left field, with Rudy Law in center and Harold Baines in right. Maybe the blend of sun and suds got too potent, but the fans in left and right started chanting "Less Filling!" and "Tastes Great!" back and forth. It reminded me of the way fans in the Wrigley Field bleachers yell "Left Field Sucks!" and "Right Field Sucks!" at each other to pass the time while waiting for that long-overdue World Series appearance by the Cubs. The difference was, those Detroit fans were really smoked. They started throwing batteries, coins and other stuff at Rudy, so he went into the dugout and put on a batting helmet.

All of a sudden, the crowd started losing ugly. The chant changed to "Bulls—!" and "F—You!" They got so loud, it was deafening, and a threat to forfeit the game didn't quiet them down. Finally, the cops went in and cleared out the bleachers, all the way around from left to right, so nobody was left in those seats. It took half an hour or longer to get the game started again.

HIZZONER, MAYOR RONNIE

It might have been news to Harold Washington, the popular mayor of Chicago in 1983, but he had a rival, at least on the South Side.

"Ron Kittle was the mayor of Comiskey Park," said Chicago sportscaster Tom Shaer about the impact this

charismatic slugger made on White Sox fans. "You'd never know he was a rookie. He had boundless energy and confidence. Walk around that White Sox clubhouse in 1983 and you'd find a lot of free spirits."

"None of them were freer than Kittle. It was interesting the way he fit into that group so seamlessly.

"Baseball's got this code about rookies being seen and not heard. Sometimes that's not good. It wouldn't have been good for Kittle to keep quiet in '83, because he contributed with his bat and his personality. I respect the Sox veterans who decided to let Kitty be Kitty."

I didn't knock one into the left field stands as those who held up the "Kreem one Kittle" sign might have preferred, but I did enjoy standing on second base after a double.

K's Not O.K.

Ron Kittle's 1983 numbers would have been worth enough money to bankrupt Fort Knox if a young player racked them up now. Superstar salaries, ranging up to the $22 million a year Alex Rodriguez gets from the Yankees, would have come close to matching the entire league's player payroll not long ago. The one subpar stat in Kittle's outstanding season was his AL-leading total of 150 strikeouts.

"Home run hitters have that big arc in their swing, so they strike out a lot," said Charley Lau, the White Sox hitting guru. "Ron doesn't crawl into a hole when he does. He figures he'll get ahold of one the next time up."

Kittle kept his disappointment about those K's to himself, just like his lengthy injury list and the daily pain he quietly endured. His answer to a question about the strikeout total was typical Kittle. "I was going for the Cy Young Award," he said. "They tell me there's more money in that."

A MIND GAME

The record shows I wasn't always sensational, and I never pretended to be. Some days, I could turn on a beebee and pull it over the fence. Other times, I couldn't get my bat on a beach ball. It's mostly mental.

Hitting a baseball is one of the toughest tasks in any sport, but if you come up to the plate defeated, you'll go back to the dugout carrying your bat. Good hitters pack many shapes, sizes and styles into their swings.

What they have in common is a positive attitude. It always amazed me how guys got through long slumps, like Robin Ventura going zero for 41. I would have committed suicide, no doubt about it. I used to say my whole career seemed like a succession of one for eight, two for eight. Even so, I was one of the few hitters who could literally carry a team for a week.

HIT 'EM BACK

When I got hit by a pitch, I got up out of the dirt and took my base. The next time up against that guy, I was swinging for home runs, gappers, line drives, anything to hit the ball harder than he hit me. Harold Baines was even better. He never said a word, but after a knockdown pitch, he had the knack of lining the next pitch past the guy's ear, into center field.

Baines and Greg Luzinski were able to respond to that sort of challenge from a pitcher. So was I. Mental adjustments turn ground balls into line drives when you meet the ball squarely and into homers when you get under the pitch just a bit. I always used the same stance, drew that superstitious line with my bat and cleaned the batter's box, erasing those white lines.

Maybe I should have adjusted more, but once I got set, I hated to move my back foot. When it was planted, you could have thrown a bowling ball at me and I wouldn't move. That's why I got hit by pitches. People would ask, "Why didn't you duck?" When I was locked in on the pitcher, I didn't want to. My elbows got banged up, but I was dug in, so the pitch would hit me and drop straight down.

PITCHERS CAN BE HITTERS

Fear? Not one time in my career was I afraid of getting hit. If they threw at your head, your reflexes worked pretty doggone quick. I basically stayed in there. The good pitchers knew when to throw at a batter. With a base open, they'd bury one in your side. I didn't care, except for that one time I got hit in the knee by Mike Flanagan on a 3-0 count in the '83 playoff with the Orioles.

It was a breaking pitch and he said it got away from him, but it turned out to be more painful for the White Sox and our fans than it did for me. My knee swelled up like a balloon, and I was through for the rest of the series. Some pitchers would tell you they were going to throw at you. Mostly it was reprisal after a guy on the other team got hit.

There are unwritten rules to these games within the game, so they don't often turn into all-out brawls.

JUST WIN, BABY

"Ron Kittle and I worked well together," Tony La Russa said of his new fence-buster. "He was a winner on the field, but he usually found a way to stick a needle in here and there. He like to horse around in the clubhouse, even with strictly-business guys like Carlton Fisk. There were great personalities on the 1983 White Sox and the kidding around added to the fun we had once the early-season problems got smoothed out.

"Ron was older than some rookies. He'd already hurt his neck and had some life experiences, so he wasn't really a baby. Everybody knows he's got a very quick wit. Kitty could give and take with the best on our club and come right back at them. He didn't act like the new guy in town. If he had something funny to say, he'd say it. Some kids just up from the minors duck their heads and say, 'Well, I'm not supposed to talk back.' Not him. He was right in the middle of it all.

"One reason Ron got respect from the veterans was he didn't put on airs. He expected to succeed, and it was no surprise to him. He never changed expression after a game, so you couldn't tell if he went three for three or zero for four. I remember the day he got riled up after striking out in Cleveland, and I had to take him out of the game.

That wasn't typical of Kittle's stable demeanor. He carried himself well—didn't get too pleased or too mad, whether he got a hit or made an out. But baseball's an emotional game, so if you don't get upset at not coming through in the clutch, it means you don't care.

"I liked his patient attitude, though. You could see him thinking about some pitcher in his head: 'You got me today, but I'll get you tomorrow.' I told him in spring training that he'd have to be a complete ballplayer to fit in on our team, and that's what he turned out to be. There was some question about his fielding when he came up to the White Sox. He was an average left fielder as a rookie, sometimes better than that."

4

STARS SHINE ON COMISKEY

Kittle's in Orbit, Too

By the time we got to that laugh-it-up stage of the season, the White Sox had been through a lot. The heat we took from the media and even our fans, plus the frustration of letting some close games get away might have pulled us apart. Actually, it brought us together. I'm aware that's what all winning teams say, but things were different for us. We actually meant it.

I got all the proof I needed when I started off well while some of the established stars were spinning their wheels. Instead of giving me the cold shoulder and excluding me from the clubhouse bull sessions, they let me have my 15 minutes of fame. The media crowded around my locker, not only because I hit some transcontinental home runs, but because I was willing to talk to them every day, even when my bat hit nothing but air.

Actually, the established hitters like Greg Luzinski and Harold Baines, along with the proven pitchers, including LaMarr Hoyt and Jerry Koosman, seemed kind of relieved that they could pick and choose when to face the media firing squad. If there was any animosity toward Sox rookies, especially quotable ones, I couldn't detect it. A couple of guys from

Indiana newspapers showed up regularly, in search of Local Boy Makes Good stories, and I was happy to oblige them. A lot of my pals made frequent treks to Comiskey Park, along with guys I had played with and against in high school at Gary Wirt. It was fun to gab with them before the game, pose for pictures, sign autographs and cut up old touches.

Five of my high school classmates had seats in the first row, right at the left-field wall. They were there for me every day. When Rickey Henderson came to town, they'd throw pennies, nickels, dimes, quarters at him, drink beer and root like crazy. I'll have to get together with those guys and tell them how good it made me feel to have my own cheerleaders. And Rickey didn't mind. He'd pick up the money, smile and wave at the fans. He probably still has that change in his pocket. One of the most gratifying things was seeing my old coaches, good people like Jerry Troxel and Ken Schreiber, La Porte High's baseball coach for 38 years, coming out to watch me play and telling the Chicago reporters about the way I worked to get this chance. I was having the time of my life, and just when I thought things couldn't get any better, the All-Star publicity buildup began.

THIS DREAM'S FOR REAL

The White Sox really spent a lot of time, money and effort to make this 50th anniversary Dream Game a dream come true. It sure was for me when I learned that I would be the only Sox player on the American League roster. For a couple of days before the game, I ran around shaking hands and collecting autographs from the Hall of Famers the White Sox brought in to honor, especially the ones who played in the first All-Star game at Comiskey Park on July 6, 1933. It was a neat touch to play the Golden Anniversary game on the same field, exactly 50 years later to the day.

I was sitting in the dugout in the early innings, still lit up like a Christmas tree from the ovation our fans gave me when the teams lined up along the baselines to be introduced. Couldn't wait to get into the lineup and become part of an All-Star box score. Except for getting listed in the starting lineup for a World Series game, I can't imagine a bigger thrill—at least in baseball. Finally, Harvey Kuenn, the American League manager, said, "All right, Kittle, you go to left field. Rickey Henderson, take over in right." That's what I wanted to hear. Left field was my personal patch of Comiskey Park turf. My Northwest Indiana buddies were packed into the bleachers, waiting to give me another big welcome.

So Henderson piped up, "Hey, Skip, I can't play right field, cuz I'm left-handed." Huh? It's true that Henderson was one of those rare players who batted right and threw left, but everybody wondered, "What did he just say?" That's Rickey, though. He went to left field. I wasn't worried about the unfamiliar sun in right. What the hell, if a spaceship had zoomed out of the clouds and hit me on the head, I wouldn't have noticed. I was already in orbit, just soaking up the electricity from those 43,801 raving maniacs in the stands.

CUBS VS. SOX

I singled my first time up off Pascual Perez of the Braves, a hard-hit ball that should have gone through to left field. Somehow, shortstop Dickie Thon of the Astros got over in the hole, made a terrific stop and bullet throw, but I beat it out. Whenever I see the tape of that play, I wonder how anybody ever gets a hit in the major leagues.

Defenses are so good on that level, they'll catch the ball unless you hit it out of sight.

But what really got the fans going was my next trip, with Lee Smith of the Cubs pitching for the NL.

Power against power, Sox against Cubs. Lee and I were friends, but I called out to him, "I'm coming after you, pal." Smitty just nodded, because the crowd's roar had him as juiced up as I was.

That was one time I really tried to hit one over the roof. Comiskey would have gone bananas, but he struck me out on a high fastball. On the way back to the dugout, I heard the man with the radar gun say, "That last pitch was 103 miles per hour." After the game, some writer asked why I couldn't catch up with a pitch like that. I told him, "When they get past 95, it's out of my league." But when you're caught up in the kind of atmosphere we had all through that All-Star game, pure adrenaline takes over. I hit some balls into the light towers during batting practice. The thing I couldn't help noticing that with the crowd going wild on every pitch, even the veterans were getting fired up. I can only imagine what it would have been like if the 1983 White Sox had played a World Series game in Comiskey Park.

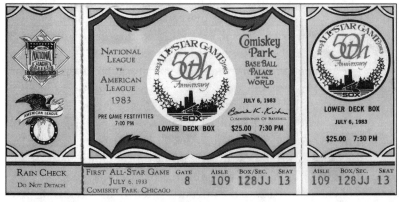

Representing the White Sox in the 1983 All-Star Game at Comiskey Park was a huge thrill. The game was played on the same field—50 years to the day after—as the first All-Star game in 1933.

STILL A HIT WHEN HE MISSES

> *"A lot of guys are happy to talk after they've made the game-winning play, no matter what sport it is," said veteran radio and TV sportscaster Les Grobstein, one of the hardest-working and most knowledgeable observers of the Chicago sporting scene. It's just human nature, I guess, but Ron Kittle was an exception to that rule. He was a terrific interview, win or lose. After Lee Smith of the Cubs struck him out in the 1983 All-Star game, Ron told us, "He was gonna hump back and throw and I was gonna hump back and swing for the roof. Lee won this one."*

ANOTHER CALLED SHOT?

I was sitting on the dugout steps before Fred Lynn of the Red Sox came to bat with the bases loaded in the third inning of the All-Star game. Attlee Hammaker, was pitching for the NL. Lynn had never seen Hammaker before, but I played against him him in Triple-A ball, so I told Freddie, "This guy likes to start lefty batters off with a breaking ball."

Sure enough, Hammaker's first pitch was a curve, and Lynn whacked it into the right-field seats for the only grand slam homer in All-Star history. Comiskey already was rocking, but it turned into a madhouse when we scored seven runs in that inning, another All-Star record. The rest of that 13-3 laugher for the AL was almost as much fun on the South Side as the night when the White Sox clinched the 1959 pennant.

Lynn came back to the dugout so excited, he was kissing people. I played golf with him a while ago, and he's still talking about what a feeling it was that night.

5

WINNING UGLY'S
BEAUTIFUL

1983 Reasons for Sox-cess

Along with me, most fans thought Doug Rader, manager of the Texas Rangers, slapped that "Winnin' Ugly" label on the White Sox out of sheer frustration. Actually, the Red Rooster was smarter than that.

The Rangers led the Western Division by a microscopic half-game over California on July 11, exactly halfway through the 1983 schedule. It was a four-team race at that, with the Rangers, Angels, Kansas City Royals and Sox bunched closer than a Chicago election before the tombstone votes get counted.

We shoved the Rangers out of the top spot on July 18, and the only thing that changed from there to the finish line was the distance between the White Sox and the rest of the West, floundering in our wake. We already were ahead by six and a half games on August 19, the eve of a Comiskey Park doubleheader against the Rangers. That's when Rader unleashed some psychological warfare, declaring that the Sox were "Winnin' Ugly" and we wouldn't be able to stay with our division rivals now that the race was beginning to heat up.

It wasn't as catchy a slogan as "Remember the Alamo," but I guess the Rooster figured that was already taken in Texas, so he did the best he could. And even though the Sox swept the next day's twin bill and won three of four in the series, that ferocious competitor refused to surrender.

"The White Sox have decent pitching and not much else," he growled on the way out of town. "I still expect to see their bubble bust."

SHADES OF 1969

In a touch of irony that caused some Cub fans with long memories to mutter into their beer, veteran Sox left-hander Jerry Koosman racked up his 200th career victory in the second game of the doubleheader sweep that knocked Texas out of the race. They recalled Koosman, still a winner at 40, as a starter for the New York Mets juggernaut that roared down the stretch in 1969, flattening the Cubs, ending the pennant dreams of delirious North Siders and going on humiliate the Baltimore Orioles in the World Series.

"We never worried about the Cubs for a minute," Koosman said of those Amazin' Mets. "Our only concern was the way we were playing."

Koosman proved to be a big plus on the mound and in the clubhouse, mentoring younger White Sox pitchers, in 1983. "I can still pitch," the steady veteran said. "Best of all, I enjoy helping the kids get ready for their first play-off." Sure enough, Koosman was the starter on September 17, when the Sox clinched the division crown. Manager Tony La Russa saved the ultimate accolade for the aging warrior.

"Kooz doesn't pitch old," he said.

WINNING'S VERY PRETTY

Doug Rader had to agree that winning ugly sure beats the alternative. The Texas manager finally flew the white flag when his Rangers came to Comiskey Park to lose a two-game series in late August, helping the White Sox coast through the final month. After starting 1983 with three straight setbacks to Rader's team, the Sox whipped them in eight of the next 10 showdowns, and "Winnin' Ugly" was the in word in Chicago.

"They made all the plays tonight," Rader conceded to the media after Richard Dotson's three-hitter toppled Texas 2-1, with a Comiskey crowd of 33,987 gleefully hurling ugly remarks in his direction. "I'd like to win some ugly games. What I said about the White Sox was just sour grapes. I didn't say winning ugly was bad. Anyway, you guys sure had fun with it."

Maybe Rader had a legitimate beef in a couple of the Rangers' losses to the Sox. I recall one game when we beat them because Tom Paciorek got jammed by a pitch and somehow dinked it over the first baseman's head. The ball hit the foul line, they made two bad relay throws and Wimpy came all the way around. The next day, we trailed by a run with Dave Stewart pitching for Texas. With two on, Rudy Law squibbed a little comebacker to the mound. Stewart grabbed it, ran to first base, stepped on the bag and then spiked the ball over his head. Luckily for us, Dave thought it was the third out.

So our guys are running around the bases while Stewart figures out the inning isn't over. He picks up the ball, makes a wild throw, both runs come across and we win again. We couldn't even hit the ball past the pitcher, but that's what happens when the breaks are going your way. Baseball really is a crazy game at times. Speaking of crazy, Rader cut loose with a blanktey-blank winnin' ugly White Sox tirade after that game. But Dave Stewart handled it like a pro and learned from his mistake.

Just to show there were no hard feelings, Tony La Russa hired Rader as his third-base coach in 1986. In a touch of irony,

Rader, who grew up in suburban Chicago, became interim manager of the Sox when La Russa got fired in June, handling the club for two games before turning the reins over to Jim Fregosi.

JOCK'S ON HIM

Dave Stewart and I were buddies when we played together in the minor leagues. Our mutual respect did not diminish when we faced each other in the big time. So I understood what Dave was going through during a highly publicized incident.

Mistaking the number of outs wasn't the most embarrassing thing that ever happened to Dave. When he was with Oakland, he got arrested in a car with someone he expected was a shady lady. It turned out to be a transvestite, although some of his teammates in the hotel bar agreed he looked like a Hollywood glamour girl.

Later, there was some understandable bad blood between A's and White Sox when La Russa left us and became Oakland's manager. Stewart was quoted in the papers as saying, "Only a couple of guys in that (Sox) clubhouse can carry my jockstrap—Harold Baines, Carlton Fisk and Ron Kittle."

The next time I walked up to my locker, somebody had draped a giant jockstrap across the front and filled it with plastic wiffle balls. We all laughed about that, but I still appreciated the compliment. Dave included me with the guys who tried to play the game right.

SOX FEVER HITS THE ROAD

When the White Sox started hitting and pitching the way we knew we could, it didn't take long for the fans to break out with a case of pennant fever. They were awesome at home, which is one reason I hated to see old Comiskey Park go. The sound in that place was tremendous, and Nancy Faust knew how to get the crowd revved up. A few chords from her organ and the place would be rocking. When the first half ended, we weren't buried in the standings, so it didn't take long for the Sox to move up.

Just like that, more fans started greeting us in every city we traveled to. More Sox caps in the stands, waving when we got a hit, more people standing around in hotel lobbies and airports, waiting for the team bus to pull up. Collectors, autograph hounds, just plain Chicago fans making trips with us. We were seeing lots of familiar faces around the country. I began to feel like the Yankees do now or back when they had Mickey Mantle and Roger Maris in the great home run chase. You almost had to become a recluse to eat a meal in peace on the road. Fans sent cards, flowers and dinner invitations to our rooms. Tickets to Sox games were hard to get in any AL stadium. It was a great ride.

And the best part was going to other ballparks, confident we were going to win in front of a mostly hostile crowd. That was even true in Texas, where they had some of the ugliest face masks you ever saw, all wearing White Sox caps. The uglier the better, because we enjoyed sending those fans home in an ugly mood.

NOT ALL FUN AND GAMES

People get so worked up about which team wins or loses a ballgame, it sometimes takes a real scare to keep things in perspective. We got one the night Greg Luzinski was batting and I stood in the on-deck circle. This little girl, about three or four years old, cute as a button, was standing up on her front-row seat, clapping and having a good time. Bull broke his bat with a big swing and the jagged end came flying over my head. I'll

Comiskey Park fans broke out with a serious case of pennant fever in 1983. As we shot up the standings, tickets became harder and harder to come by. Signing autographs for some younger White Sox faithful was a nightly task.

never forget trying to block it with my bat and turning around to see the little girl falling.

Her feet hit the floor just as Luzinski's bat slammed into her seat like a spear and stuck there. She would have been killed for sure, but the pointed end just missed her. Along with her parents, Greg was in shock until I told them, "She's O.K." Julio Cruz came over and gave the kid a bat, but it took a couple of innings for our hearts to stop pounding.

No Burnout, Day or Night

The White Sox had plenty of depth, another reason why we didn't fold after the All-Star break. Some of the '69 Cubs complained that their crusty manager, Leo Durocher, didn't rest his regulars enough, so they wore down under the hot sun in all those day games. Tony La Russa had plenty of confidence in the reserves, so nobody played the full 162-game schedule. Harold Baines was tops for us, appearing in 156.

There was no reason to wear anybody down. Pudge Fisk had a capable backup behind the plate in Booter Hill. Any of our first basemen, Greg Walker, Tom Paciorek and Mike Squires, could have been front-liners on other clubs. With Scotty Fletcher and Jerry Dybzinski rotating at shortstop, that position stabilized. Vance Law needed only sporadic relief at third base, where La Russa delightedly defied one of baseball's oldest traditions by letting left-handed Squires appear in one game there, though he had no chances. The outfield was mostly set, with me in left field, Rudy Law in center and Baines in right. Bull Luzinski's 32 homers and 95 RBIs earned him the AL's DH of the Year laurels.

Starters Can't Stop

The starting pitchers came on so strong that La Russa was able to kid about it when the Sox had the race well in hand. LaMarr Hoyt (24) and Richard Dotson combined for 46 of the team's 99 victories, the highest two-man total since Eddie Cicotte (29) and Claude Williams (23) racked up 52 wins for the infamous 1919 Black Sox.

With speculation about his rotation for the upcoming playoffs on the fans' minds, the manager "confessed" to a startled reporter that he had a serious concern about those starters.

Sensing a scoop, the scribe's eyebrows shot up like the Comiskey Park scoreboard's firecracker salute to a home team home run. "What's that, Tony?" he asked, pencil poised.

"They're just pitching too darn well," La Russa replied. "I can't get my bullpen enough work to stay sharp."

THE KITTLE'S BOILING

I enjoyed making our home crowds happy, but when we won a game in the ninth inning and the fans rushed onto the field to join the celebration—remember, this was when they ran out of the stands only to congratulate us, not to slug players, coaches or umpires—I wouldn't come out of the dugout to join in.

Everybody remembers the mob scene when Julio Cruz jumped on home plate with the winning run to clinch our division crown. I was probably one of the last people out there. Inside, I was jumping as high as Juice Cruz or anybody else, except I'm not the type to bang the drums.

There never was a day when I went to any ballpark, from high school to Comiskey, when I didn't want to be the guy who won the game. That mental attitude is as important as talent, sometimes even more so.

When I played against guys who thought talking tough really made them tough, I countered them with humor, fun and sarcasm. Talking doesn't get it done. We got it done on the 1983 White Sox by doing a lot of little things right, over and over.

When you see the payoff for all that effort, it chokes you up, even if you don't care to put it on public display. Sure, I wanted to win, I hated to lose, and either way, I can't be a cheerleader. Winning is something you should expect of yourself, or the way my dad, Slim Kittle, looked at it, you should demand of yourself. I'd prefer to accept victory like a professional, without taunting the losers, and handle defeat as gracefully as possible.

LaMarr Hoyt, the ace of our White Sox staff, cranks it up. LaMarr won 24 games for us during the regular season, and one more against Baltimore in the playoffs.

REGGIE STROKES KITTY

Nobody enjoyed the media spotlight more than Hall of Famer Reggie Jackson, the superstar slugger who once performed a World Series feat not even Babe Ruth could match. Sure, Ruth called his shot against the Cubs in the 1932 World Series, slamming a home run into the Wrigley Field bleachers at the exact spot where he'd just pointed with his 58-ounce bat after taking two called strikes from Charley Root.

But Jackson topped him by hitting three Yankee Stadium homers on three consecutive pitches against the Dodgers in the 1977 fall classic. Flamboyant Jackson's 10 round-trippers in 27 World Series games earned him a permanent place in baseball history as "Mr. October."

By 1983, the 37-year-old Jackson was playing for the California Angels, relishing his status as one of baseball's elder statesmen, especially on topics like bashing baseballs for long distances. So when rookie Ron Kittle began rocketing homers all over the AL, it was natural for Reggie to have his say about the inevitable comparisons by media and fans alike between his accomplishments and Kittle's potential.

"Let him go, man," Jackson said. "Let Ron Kittle have some fun and keep doing his own thing, instead of pestering him to death. Don't start in with that stuff about 'He's on pace to catch Ruth or Aaron or Jackson' or anybody else. Why put that pressure on him? Kittle wants to murder the ball every time he's up to bat, so just see what he can do, instead of hanging that target on him to hit 40 or 50 home runs a year.

"If he's as good as he looks now, it won't be long before everybody wants a piece of him. Remember, the higher up a tree a monkey climbs, the more you can see his tail. So let Kittle hit homers at his own pace and don't try to make him into somebody else."

BOOM! ZAP! POW!

Even with our great pitching, it was the offensive explosion triggering those scoreboard fireworks that fired up the fans, packed Comiskey Park every night and grabbed some overdue headlines for the South Siders. Carlton Fisk's bat came alive,

Rudy Law ran wild for a club-record 77 stolen bases and the rest of the hitters found their groove.

For Greg Luzinski, it was more like a missile-launching silo. The Bull put three Comiskey Park roofshots into orbit in 1983 before I found the range with a pair. Such prodigious pokes had the whole town talking, and the rest of the country soon joined in.

THE PAYBACK YEAR

I got rewarded for hanging in there with a lifetime of memories in just one season. That was 1983, a magical year for the White Sox, for me and especially for the city of Chicago. Winning was what we needed around here, and I'm talking about the working people I grew up with, not the players or the owners.

I'll always feel proud that the White Sox started Chicago off on a long victory streak. The Cubs broke their playoff dry spell in 1984, the Bears won the Super Bowl a little later and then Michael Jordan and the Bulls came along to build that NBA dynasty. I know how hard it is to win one championship in any sport. But six world titles in the same decade? Fantastic, and still hard to believe, but the whole town went wild and we all felt better about ourselves. Winning can do wonderful things for players and fans alike.

RIGHT TIME, RIGHT TOWN

That unforgettable year, 1983, in that wonderful city, Chicago, was my own personal field of dreams. In the fall of 2004, I went with a dozen motorcycle guys from Indiana on a trip to the ballfield in Iowa where they made that *Field of Dreams* movie. It's a guy thing. No chicks allowed!

At the field they have balls and gloves and I ended up throwing batting practice for just about everyone who was there that day, including several fathers with their young children. One of my motorcycle buddies was warming up and swinging full speed. When he came up he pointed to the outfield and said it was his dream to hit a home run into the corn.

Now this field is very short—the corn at the end of the outfield is only about 200 feet away from the plate. So I told him my dream was to drill him in the side for taking a full swing with kids and families running around. So that's what I did. He got the point. At least I hope so.

I recently visited the cornfield in Iowa where they filmed *Field of Dreams.* I pitched batting practice and nailed a friend who swung the bat too hard with children around.

From Northwest Indiana to Iowa and back, we rode for five days. It was like the camaraderie I had with the guys when I played, just shooting the breeze and talking baseball with my buddies. Sitting around and telling the same story over and over again, each time the story gets better and better than the year before. Is it that we forget the real stories or just make the old stories seem better? Funny how that works as we get older and greyer.

We came back bruised and full of bugs, but it was fun. At the field, they even took pictures of us wearing White Sox jerseys, coming out of the cornstalks and onto the field. No, I didn't pretend to be Shoeless Joe Jackson. It was enough to recall the memories of being Ron Kittle, left fielder for the 1983 Chicago White Sox.

Talent alone is not enough to put anybody's name on a big-league roster. I played with and against guys in the minors who had more raw ability than me. They could outhit, outrun and outplay me, but they couldn't outwork me. That's how I made it, with effort, a high tolerance for pain, plus a little luck and a helping hand from some good people. My dad told me, "As hard as you think you are working, someone is working harder." I will never forget that.

SHOWTIME AT COMISKEY

The one thing that sticks out most about 1983 is how much fun it was to walk into the clubhouse every day. Without the winning, I guess things would have been a lot different. With it, going to work turned into a 24/7 party. The only unhappy note for me was the last one. I wanted the music to keep playing, especially Nancy Faust on the organ, turning Comiskey Park into a zoo with her "Na-Na-Na-Na, Hey, Hey, Hey, Goodbye" salute to pitchers kayoed by the Sox and visitors we beat.

The way we played in the second half of 1983 created the sweetest sound I ever heard—the roar from thousands of our fans, bouncing off the walls of that beat-up old ballpark. The place was like Chicago to me. Tough times only made it tougher and good times only made it more fun.

In 1983, every game the White Sox played turned into a memory. Fans never stop wanting to talk to me about that season. So many unexpected possibilities opened up, it was almost like a dream coming true.

We were kicking butt—a 50-16 record from July 26 on. (That's a virtually unheard-of .757 percentage, especially for such a long stretch). Pretty remarkable. Everybody was a White Sox fan, if only for that summer. I can't tell you how many times people walk up to me in restaurants or the mall to say, "Hey, Ron, that was a magical year."

GOPHER BROKE, RON

I was a better outfielder than some people gave me credit for. When a player has early success in the big leagues, there's usually a quick buildup, comparing him with all kinds of players, and then the media starts looking for holes in his game. I had some good games on defense, but there was the night in Comiskey Park when I got outfoxed by a gopher.

Hitters are always glad to see a pitcher serve them up a gopher ball, the old expression for a pitch they hit out of the park, but I sure wasn't happy when this live gopher and that bouncing baseball found themselves on a collision course.

We were playing the Detroit Tigers at Comiskey Park on August 4. Lou Whitaker led off the first inning for the Tigers with a line drive down the left-field line. I went over to cut it off, and I swear this is what happened—a gopher scampered out in front of the ball. It hit him on the head, bounced over my glove and rolled into the corner while Whitaker took third base.

He got a double and I got an error, but I don't know why the official scorer couldn't see that darned gopher. It should have been recorded as the first triple ever on a gopher ball, although I was upset because we lost the game 6-3, not on account of the error.

When the writers came in the clubhouse after the game, I told them about the gopher, but I guess they didn't believe me, either. One asked if I'd heard the fans booing me for letting Whitaker's hit get away. "Yeah, I did, but I was too busy yelling at the gopher to explain to them," I said.

Dot's Good, Kitty

Ron Kittle's defensive ability got much better reviews on September 23, especially from Richard Dotson.

The White Sox starter won his 20th game that night, beating the California Angels, 3-1. The right-hander joined LaMarr Hoyt in that charmed circle, giving the Sox their first pair of 20-game winners in the same season since Wilbur Wood and Jim Kaat in 1974.

"Without Kitty's defense, I couldn't have done it tonight," Dotson said, gleefully soaking up a spray of celebratory champagne. "And without the way our defense backed me up all season, I'd be having the usual postgame beer now, instead of 20-game champagne."

Two sparkling plays by the Sox left fielder in Anaheim Stadium made the difference for Dotson. In the third inning, racing full tilt toward the foul line, Kittle made a sprawling, back-handed stab of Rod Carew's sinking liner. It saved at least one run, with Angels runner Dick Schofield on third base and two out. If the drive had eluded Kittle's dive, the speedy Carew could have turned it into an inside-the-park homer, knotting the score at 2-2. Then, with two on and two out in the home seventh and Dotson clinging to a 2-1 edge, Gary Pettis singled to left. California's third-base coach, Preston Gomez, waved run-

ner Jerry Narron around. But Kittle pounced on the hit and fired a one-hop strike to catcher Carlton Fisk, who slapped the inning-ending, rally-killing, game-saving tag on the sliding Narron.

"The defensive star," chirped Sox manager Tony La Russa, pounding a congratulatory clenched fist with Kittle. "Say, Kitty, when did you think you'd ever hear that?" asked Fisk with a sly grin. But the old pro receiver had been knocked dizzy by many runners while stretching for bad throws to the plate, so he always appreciated a good one.

"It took a perfect peg to get Narron, and that's what Kittle gave me," Fisk told the media.

GLIMPSE OF HEAVEN

"You have to spend some time in purgatory before the heavenly gates open," Roland Hemond said when it became clear in August that the 1983 White Sox were a runaway freight train, rumbling toward the promised land of playoff nirvana. "Well, they're opening now for us."

"When the club got hot, it stayed hot, winning the West by 20 games," Hemond said, reflecting back on a season that had been, and remains, one of the most satisfying in his career, spanning more than a half-century in baseball. "The White Sox kept hearing they couldn't win with Ron Kittle and other rookies in the lineup, and they proved the critics were wrong. Tony La Russa said we didn't stand a chance unless Carlton Fisk and Greg Luzinski started hitting the way they could. Kittle's bat and charisma helped keep us together until that happened. Combined with a solid pitching staff, the consistency of Harold Baines, Rudy Law's 77 stolen bases and strong defense, especially after we traded for Julio Cruz to play second base, it was a winning blend.

"Winning is always fun, but with Kittle around, it was even more enjoyable. Ron would come out with some

*remark that made people think, 'Where's he coming from?'
and then he found a humorous way to fit it right into the
conversation. One winter night, I remember going to the
annual White Sox fan club dinner in Coal City, Illinois,
Kittle drove in all the way from Gary, Indiana, to be there
on a snowy night. He got up and said, 'It took me three and
a half hours to find this God-forsaken town.' The people
were kind of shocked, but by the time Ron was through
talking, everybody was laughing and they loved him.
That's the way Kittle's personality comes through. He
started off knocking the town, and a little while later, he
owned the town."*

NA, NA, HEY, HEY—GOOD SOX

*From her perch in the Comiskey Park organist's booth,
Nancy Faust could see White Sox fans and players coming
together in a crescendo of victory fervor and playoff fever.
A fan as well as a student of the game, Nancy made some
perceptive observations and on-the-money predictions as
the summer of '83 rolled along to its emotional climax.*

*"Now everybody's into the game," she said when the
Sox turned on the heat after the All-Star break.*

*"When the other team makes an out, there's a sigh of
relief in the stands. The night we clinch, these fans will go
absolutely berserk. I'm playing songs now, like 'I'm a
Believer' and 'One Step Closer' that I've never had to use
before. This is the good old days, right now. People will
still be talking about this season 20 years from now." As
usual, she was right.*

THE BRIGHTEST NIGHT

We clinched a tie for the Western Division title on
September 16, so it was just a matter of time until the party

started. "It's been what, 24 years since our last party?" clubhouse man Willie Thompson wanted to know, flashing back to when the White Sox won the 1959 AL pennant. "This one might go on for 10 years."

Well, not quite. At least the clincher happened in Comiskey Park the very next night, allowing a hysterical, overflow Comiskey Park throng of Sox fans to celebrate with us. It had been a few weeks since we played a game that packed any emotional punch, because the title was wrapped up by the end of our bombs-away 22-9 August spree. Willie had plastic wrap in place to protect clubhouse lockers, but with 200 bottles of champagne flowing, everybody and everything else in the place got soaked. We lost a 3-1 lead to Seattle in the ninth inning, but before the fans stopped groaning, Harold Baines's sacrifice fly sent Juice Cruz romping home to stomp on the plate, beat the Mariners 4-3 and touched off total ecstasy on the South Side.

"We're the champions," Tony La Russa said, his usual all-business game face drenched in champagne and an emotional tear or two. "Think about that. Not New York or Los Angeles. Chicago!"

Even though I was probably the last man off the bench when Cruz crossed the plate and jubilant fans spilled out of the stands to join the White Sox in a group hug, I was just as happy as everybody else. I didn't stand at the plate to admire my home runs when I hit them or trash-talk the victimized pitcher while I circled the bases. It's just not in my nature to get overly emotional, so I didn't try to match Juice Cruz's exuberance when the White Sox won or sit brooding at my locker and scowling at the media after we lost. I got mad at myself if I didn't come through in the clutch, but even when I was a kid, just learning to compete, I left the cheerleading to others. Anyway, it was obvious this party would last until the sun came up next morning, so I stuck around for a while and then drove home to Indiana.

But the clubhouse scene was pretty wild. Roland Hemond, a favorite target of the champagne sprayers, didn't mind a bit. The wrinkled suit he wore that night later got framed and displayed outside the Bards Room, where the media dined in old Comiskey Park. I remember Roland telling us, "This kind of night might happen only once in your lifetime, so enjoy it." We did. Even Greg Luzinski, normally not one to let down his hair in public, was like a kid under the Christmas tree. His champagne somehow seemed to get sprayed wherever the sportswriters were struggling in vain to scribble quotes in their drenched notebooks, and Bull kept bellowing, "How long has it been?"

MILD ABOUT HARRY

A born diplomat, White Sox general manager Roland Hemond offered a tactful rebuke to the skeptics who couldn't imagine they would wind up as baseball's biggest winner in the 1983 regular season with a 99-63 mark, second highest victory total in club history.

The AL East champ, Baltimore, breathed down their necks at 98-64. In the midst of that we-showed-you clubhouse jubilation on clinching night, Hemond kept things in perspective, asking only, "Where are the detractors now?"

In sharp contrast, Sox chairman Jerry Reinsdorf couldn't resist the temptation to take a double-barreled potshot at Harry Caray and Jimmy Piersall, the tempestuous former Sox broadcast team. Their partnership had imploded over what Reinsdorf and Sox president Eddie Einhorn considered unfair criticism by that flamboyant duo. "Wherever you're at, Harry and Jimmy, eat your hearts out," Reinsdorf said between sips and sprays of champagne. "I hope people realize what scum you are."

ASPIRIN, ANYONE?

Nobody was mad at anybody, not even Cub fans, if they were White Sox fans that night. The celebration was going strong in Northwest Indiana strongholds of Sox supporters. Fortunately, enough players, including me, got enough sleep to be ready for the next day's strictly for exercise game against the Mariners. That didn't include everybody on the roster, by any means. When I got to the clubhouse, some of the guys straggling in looked like they'd spent the night in a doorway on Madison Street. Tony La Russa was wandering around with an uncharacteristic pregame smile, calling for volunteers to totter onto the field.

"I had a list of probables, but now it's down to barely possibles," Tony said. "When I left the party at 4 a.m., a lot of people were blocking punts with their faces." Even so, we somehow beat Seattle 6-0 behind Rich Dotson, stretching our home victory streak to a club-record 17 straight. Nobody remembers the details, but Sox players and fans alike went home in awe of Mike Squires. Spanky, a good glove man who played a first-rate first base backup role, went down in baseball trivia history as one of the few left-handers to appear in a big-league box score as a catcher. What the Comiskey Park crowd of 40,984 can't forget was the sight of Squires defying a stiff breeze to climb atop the right-field roof and hoist the flag proclaiming the White Sox as 1983 champions of the AL West. Spanky had been on the Sox since 1975, longer than anyone else, so he was traditionalist La Russa's logical choice for the daredevil stunt.

Besides, not many of his teammates were in shape to do anything riskier than gulp aspirin.

"It was an honor not many players get," Squires said. "I was so used to losing, I never figured this dream would come true. The Sox know I'm a role player, and they showed their appreciation by giving me a four-year contract."

La Russa likes that sort of loyalty. When Tony became the Cards' manager, he hired Squires as a scout.

A RAVE FROM DAVE

Dave Duncan, the astute White Sox pitching coach and long-time associate of Tony La Russa, summed up the 1983 season with the same insight he employed to turn that staff into a finely tuned machine.

"The night we clinched the division, everybody appreciated each other so much, it was really a neat feeling," Duncan recalled. "Back then, we had lots of team get-togethers, so we knew each other's strengths and weaknesses pretty well. Ron Kittle was an interesting guy, in a fun way. He got help with pranks and stay-loose stuff from the veterans, and yeah, Booter Hill. They always had something going on. When the team was on the road, we stayed together. The payoff was watching things come together."

"That solved all our problems, because the first half was so hard. It all clicked when the starting pitchers kept giving us outstanding games, one after another."

LOADS OF SOX APPEAL

We got support from all over Chicago when people saw the White Sox were for real. Besides the hardcore fans who were having the time of their lives, packing Comiskey Park for every game, we started getting a lot of bandwagon riders. That was fine with me. It added to the excitement while we were putting longballs from our hitters together with tremendous pitching from LaMarr Hoyt, Rich Dotson, Floyd Bannister and Britt Burns.

The fans kept coming, even though we wrapped up our first playoff shot since 1959 midway through September, with 13 games left to go. Suspense was absent, but not Sox fever, when the home schedule ended with a doubleheader sweep over the Twins on September 21. That gave us a 55-26 Comiskey Park record, along with an all-time attendance mark of 2,132,821.

Before we left for the AL championship series opener in Baltimore, a crowd of 10,000 or more swarmed into a Loop rally, surrounding the landmark Daley Center Picasso to hear mayor Harold Washington read a "White Sox Pride Day" proclamation. I fired up the fans by using a bat to break open a piñata shaped like an Oriole, showering them with souvenirs, and Greg Luzinski promised, "In four days, we're gonna have a really big party and you'll be dancing in Rush Street."

As things turned out, the pennant party had to be postponed. I wish I'd been able to use my bat more effectively on the real Orioles. When the White Sox do win it, look for me on

When tickets for our playoff series against Baltimore went on sale, fans from Northwest Indiana raced up I-94 to get tickets before they sold out. Their support is something I'll appreciate forever.

Rush Street. In honor of what didn't happen at the end in 1983, I'll be doing the Twist.

Ron Remembers

> *Tom Shaer arrived at Comiskey Park with a WGN-TV camera crew to film White Sox fans at the ticket windows, snapping up seats for the October playoff games with Baltimore.*
>
> *"It seemed like all of Northwest Indiana was in line to buy them," Shaer said. "These were Ron Kittle's people, from Gary, Munster, Valparaiso, Chesterton, wherever.*
>
> *"The first thing they said on camera was, 'We're from Kittle country.' The next day, Ron told me he'd seen it on Channel 9. He asked, 'Did you get the names of those Indiana people?'*
>
> *"He wanted to look them up in the phone book and call or write a note to thank them for their support. I found some addresses and gave them to him. How many players would take that much trouble to show their appreciation for the fans? Here's a guy who never forgot where he came from."*

Dewey "Burns" Birds

As far as I'm concerned, the story of our frustrating best-of-five playoff with the Orioles was the way Dewey LaMarr Hoyt pitched in Game 1 and the gem he didn't get to pitch in Game 5. There was no Game 5, but don't blame that on Britt Burns, who threw a nine-inning shutout in Game 4, busting his hump and pitching his heart out to get us there. We couldn't score a run to beat Baltimore that afternoon and reach a one-game series showdown, with the American League pennant on the line. If only we had, setting up a winner-take-all situation before a frenzied Comiskey Park mob, with Hoyt on the mound for the White Sox, what wouldn't I give to be in the lineup that night? Name it, and you can have it.

Chances are I would not have been able to play, or even pinch hit, even if there had been a fifth and deciding game. My knee was swollen so badly I could barely walk, let alone dig in at the plate to swing a bat. Orioles lefty Mike Flanagan unleashed a 3-2 curve in Game 3 and it nailed me in the one place where maximum damage was possible—my left kneecap. I went down, through for the series and the year.

When I returned to the ballpark the next day, hobbling on crutches, it was obvious I couldn't play. So I sat on the bench, an IV jug draining fluid from the puffed-up knee, and watched our wonderful season end.

Things happen in uncontrollable ways, so I can't make this nightmare come out the way it should have.

Both teams knew the survivor of our playoff would win the World Series, and that's what happened. It wasn't the White Sox, because we didn't get the chance. Flanagan swore he didn't throw at me on purpose. I'm still convinced that he did, but there's nothing I can do about it.

The last impression I want to leave with White Sox fans about the 1983 season is that we went out whining and crying, like sore losers. The AL playoff was there for us to take, especially behind the superb pitching of Hoyt and Burns, and we just didn't get a few clutch hits at the right moments. That's all there was to it. The Orioles had outstanding pitching, and they won the series, three games to one. The Sox were stymied by Storm Davis in the finale, matching Burns's string of scoreboard zeroes, innings after inning.

Sitting on the bench and watching, I couldn't help flashing back to Opening Day 1983, when I hit a two-run homer off the same Davis who was tying Sox bats in knots this time. Just one of those runs would have been enough for hard-luck Burns on October 8. That's baseball—joy and pain in the same package.

SIGHT FOR SAD EYES

Roland Hemond, the White Sox general manager, was standing outside Comiskey Park before Game 4 of the playoffs, stoking his natural optimism. Despite an 11-1 drubbing by the Orioles a few hours earlier, Hemond knew the Sox should win the decisive game behind ace LaMarr Hoyt, if they could even the series on this raw Saturday afternoon. Then he spotted slugger Ron Kittle across the street, and his spirits sank.

"I was devastated," Hemond said. "Kittle was hobbling on crutches, in obvious pain, dragging his left leg. I said, 'Ron are you putting me on?' He told me, 'No, Roland, this is the best I can do.' That's as close as we came to the 1983 World Series. The Baltimore people knew if they had to face Hoyt again in Game 5, they were in deep trouble.

"We never got there. Seeing Kittle like that was heartbreaking."

ORIOLES GET HOYT

LaMarr Hoyt didn't have to throw at any of the Orioles to cage them 2-1 in our Baltimore playoff opener. He was masterful. We missed lots of scoring chances, but nobody thought much of it, because if there was one thing this Sox squad could do, it was hit.

Sadly, that's the one thing we didn't do in losing the remaining three games. Hoyt was the key to our success all year, and the fans loved this pudgy wizard, too.

"LaMarr doesn't let the game get complicated," said his catcher, Carlton Fisk. "He just throws strikes, but he'll never make an underwear commercial with Jim Palmer."

LOTS OF SPOTS

"My secret was not looking for one spot to hit, like most pitchers," Hoyt said. *"I'd sneak backdoor sliders on the outside corner, high or low.*

"I fed off Richard Dotson, because his speed and control had batters leaning on changeups all night. But just being on the 1983 White Sox was the pinnacle of my career. It was the only club I ever played for that had no cliques. And Ron Kittle was the loosest rookie I ever saw.

"Some writers said he wasn't a good outfielder, but he batted in a heck of a lot more runs (100) for us than he let in for the other team."

BALTIMORE LITE

Maybe our big mistake in Game 2 was swinging away at Mike Boddicker, instead of shortening up on that dancing sinker he called his fosh ball. He changed speeds well, struck out 14 and shut us out, 4-0. We never did get back in the groove.

For a guy with such control, it seemed strange that he hit Bull Luzinski and Tom Paciorek with pitches. Roland Hemond told me Luzinski couldn't extend his arms after Boddicker nailed him on the elbow, and he went two for 15 in the series. For me, Game 2 will go down as the one where a Baltimore fan hit me—with a cup of beer.

I was chasing Cal Ripken's drive at the wall in left when I got doused, right in the face, and the ball bounced away for a double. I came back to the dugout, soaking wet and mad, but Booter Hill knew how to ease the tension, as always. He came over, licked my cheek and said, "Don't worry, Kitty. It's lite beer."

They still should have called Ripken out, because this was a fair ball, unlike the Moises Alou play at Wrigley Field in the 2003 playoffs that got the Cubs and their fans so uptight.

BEANBALL BATTLES

There was no such thing as warnings from the umpires and automatic ejections for hitting batters back in 1983. It wouldn't have done the White Sox any good, because we were trailing 4-1 when Flanagan hit me with what our fans thought was retaliation for Rich Dotson pitching high and tight to Eddie Murray of the Orioles. Flanagan was sending a message, all right, although he couldn't have done more damage to my left knee if he'd walked up to the plate and hit me with a bat.

What I called Flanagan couldn't be printed in a family newspaper, but too many people grabbed me before I could get to the mound and deliver my message in person. I went to first base, and soon had to leave the game with the knee swelling fast. That's when revenge is mandatory.

"Tony La Russa and I talked about who I should hit," Dotson admitted. "We decided Cal Ripken was the one." La Russa issued the standard postgame managerial denial, but Ripken, one of baseball's classiest people, knew how to play that game. "If Tony said Dotson wasn't throwing at me, then he wasn't," Ripken shrugged.

So it remained for La Russa to put things in perspective. "It all depends on the point of view," he said. "If they throw inside to your batter, they're trying to hit him. If your pitcher throws inside, it's part of the game."

THE FINAL OUT

Our last playoff game has been second-guessed and replayed almost as much as World War II. I think about it once in a while and talk about it when fans ask the same old questions—especially that same one old question.

Why, they always want to know, did Jerry Dybzinski round second base and keep right on going when Juice Cruz singled sharply to left field? The answer never changes and I suppose the goat horns never will be lifted from poor Jerry's head by Sox fans who can't stop replaying that agonizing moment in their own heads. The Dybber took the criticism and the blame like a man, so even the media critics had to admire the classy way he sat there and faced all comers in the silent Sox clubhouse after our season shut down with that heartbreaking 3-0 loss.

He was on first and Vance Law on second with one out in the seventh inning of a 0-0 duel when Cruz singled. Jim Leyland, coaching at third, put up the stop sign. Law stopped, but Dybzinski didn't, so he got run down and tagged out.

End of rally, and three innings later, end of season. Tito Landrum's homer off Burns in the 10th, plus two runs off relievers, sent us home and the Orioles to the World Series.

"My instincts told me to keep running, because there was going to be a play at the plate," Dybzinski said. "I was hoping they'd throw to third and get me while the run scored. It's just something I'll have to live with."

BRITT'S TRUE GRIT

"I wanted to win Game 4, not for outside approval, but for myself," said Britt Burns, the strapping left-hander who gave the White Sox an opening with his magnificent effort. *"We had such a good year in 1983, and I wanted to prove I was on the same level with LaMarr Hoyt, Floyd Bannister and Rich Dotson."*

Actually, Burns was on a level that day with Lefty Grove, Whitey Ford, Warren Spahn and other Hall of Fame southpaws. He blanked the Orioles with a five-hit, eight-strikeout masterpiece for nine and one third innings, until the unheralded Landrum stepped up with one out in the 10th.

"The first thing a pitcher has to do in a game like that is throw the ball over the plate every time," said Burns. "That exposes you to the home-run ball. I threw Landrum a fastball. He connected. It was a strike and Landum centered it with his bat. End of story. I kept the ball in the park for 120 pitches, and he got ahold of my 121st."

It was also his last. Tony La Russa walked slowly to the mound, took the ball from Burns and told him, "You know what you've done today. Don't hang your head."

"NEXT YEAR" OVERDUE

When the disappointment of the playoffs eased, I went on the Hot Stove League circuit, talking up the way the White Sox would bounce back in 1984. The fans I talked to couldn't help lamenting about what might have been, but most of them agreed we gave Chicago a lot of fun and a season to remember.

After splitting the first two playoff games in Baltimore, we felt momentum was on our side. We expected to bust loose in Comiskey Park, and those Sox fans were wild. You could taste the hunger in the air. They were ready to tear the place down for us, but this time, the Winning Ugly games went to the Orioles.

I figured if the White Sox could stay together, 1984 would be our year. We had two losses that almost everybody overlooked until they were gone—Jerry Koosman and Dick Tidrow. The fans didn't realize what kind of leaders those guys were. They'd walk up to players, poke them in the chest and say, "Hey, this is what we gotta do."

Whatever that was, it didn't get done in 1984. The White Sox were still a pretty good team, but the rest of the league improved. Our expectations of Chicago making the playoffs two years in a row came true, except that it was the Cubs, not us.

TONY'S TEAMWORK WORKS

"Things went well for the 1983 White Sox because we knew our jobs and we didn't shirk the responsibility," Tony La Russa said. "Davey Nelson talked about baserunning, Ed Brinkman about playing the infield, Dave Duncan about pitching and so on. We tried not to leave any leadership voids.

"I've managed playoff winners and World Series winners, and the '83 White Sox have a special place in my memory. Our veterans took us where we wanted to go, but new guys like Ron Kittle, Greg Walker, Scott Fletcher and Julio Cruz carried their share of the load. Besides playing well, Juice (Cruz) added some spark with his upbeat attitude. When he jumped on home plate with the run in the division title clincher, our fans went wild. To tell the truth, so did we. Chicago had been waiting a long time for a winner, and we gave them one.

"A manager always wonders if he can bring a team home in first place. Doing it with the White Sox put a cap on an unforgettable season. That champagne shower in the clubhouse was a real treat, because I didn't have anything to compare it to. Pudge Fisk had been in the 1975 World Series with the Red Sox, Jerry Koosman with the 1969 Mets and Tom Paciorek with the 1974 Dodgers. They all told me that was the most fun they had in baseball, so it's obviously something to remember. Fisk went nuts for us in the second half. Kittle and Luzinski lit up Comiskey Park with those rooftop homers, but I'd have to say our pitching got us into the playoffs.

"People still ask me where losing that fourth playoff game to the Orioles ranks on my all-time heartbreaker list. It's tied for first with the worst one—that Game 5 playoff loss to Arizona in 2001. I'll always have big regrets about both of those.

"You know, looking at the 1983 White Sox roster, nobody figured it was a championship team. What we had was a lot of heart. Kittle, Bull and a lot of other guys were

getting hits at the right time. All of a sudden, we were win-
ning, and it snowballed. LaMarr Hoyt was our stopper,
because he could throw the ball in the bottom of the strike
zone all night, so he got ground outs and we got 99 wins."

SOUTH SIDE SALUTE

I enjoyed most parts of all my 10 seasons in the big leagues.
In the minors, most players are too wrapped up in where they're
going next from where they're at, and I was no exception.
Playing for any team would have been more enjoyable without
more or less constant pain from the string of injuries that
seemed to follow me, no matter where I went.

It's undeniably true that a lot of my brightest career memories got packed into that emotionally pain-free summer of 1983
in Chicago. I remember a hit song from those days, that claimed
"...There was everything on the South Side of Chicago..." No
long-time White Sox fan can deny that. When I got together
with the other players for the 20th anniversary of the division
championship, we resumed our familiar friendly disputes about
this and that, but there was unanimous agreement on one topic.
We still share a sense of pride about the pleasure we provided for
those fantastic fans.

6

A Fine Kittle of Fisk

1983's Cast of Characters

Guys With Sox Appeal

Jerry Koosman was an unsung hero and a quiet force on the 1983 White Sox. He was like an unpaid, although definitely not unwelcome, pitching coach for the young guys on our staff. His droll sense of humor was a tonic for everyone, but the example he set really got through to pitchers like Rich Dotson, Britt Burns, Salome Barojas, Kevin Hickey and Juan Agosto. They were all searching in different ways to find their groove against big-league hitters and their most effective roles in our starting and relief rotations. Seeing the way Kooz went about things and getting words of encouragement from a man who'd been around forever was a big help to them.

I don't think any team's ever had more fun than we did in 1983. We kibitzed with Chicago sportscasters Mark Giangreco, Warner Saunders and Chet Coppock. Pictured are (from top left): Tom Paciorek, Greg Luzinski, Carlton Fisk, Vance Law and Scott Fletcher; (second row from top) myself, Giangreco and Harold Baines; (second row from bottom) Rudy Law, Coppock and Tony La Russa; (bottom row) and Julio Cruz with Saunders.

BULL'S SESSIONS PAY OFF

Tony La Russa, just beginning to see daylight in his struggle to become an established manager in the major leagues, made a giant leap forward in 1983. He was smart enough to step aside and let his veterans take a leadership role whenever the White Sox needed a morale boost. Two of them, designated hitter Greg "Bull" Luzinski and pitcher Jerry Koosman, did so behind the scenes, bringing the club together through early problems and into the late-summer breakthrough that made a shambles of the Western Division race.

"We had a combination of intriguing personalities like Ron Kittle and veterans who went out of their way to show everybody we were all in this together," La Russa said. "Koosman and Bull came from the old school. They enjoyed the game and both of them wanted everybody on the team to feel they had a part in what we were doing. The parties Kooz and Bull threw made the road seem a lot less uphill. They'd rent a suite and everybody piled in after the game for free food and lots of laughs."

"It might sound corny now, but those parties helped us get untracked. Once we did, nobody in our division was going to catch us. The coaches and the manager [La Russa, in a nostalgic mood, was talking about himself and his Sox aides—Jim Leyland, Dave Duncan, Charley Lau, Davey Nelson, Ed Brinkman and others] respected our players, and we liked them."

DEWEY DEFEATS EVERYBODY

LaMarr Hoyt, without a doubt, was The Man on our pitching staff. He was kinda dumpy and Fisk said people kept mistaking him for the equipment manager, or even worse, a sportswriter. Once he got on the mound, people learned his name in a hurry. "Lumpy" or "Catgut," he had all sorts of nicknames, but not many people remember that LaMarr's first name was Dewey.

We used to kid him about "DEWEY DEFEATS TRUMAN," that famous *Chicago Tribune* headline way back in 1948, when they jumped the gun about the winner of the presidential election. I'm not a historian, so I don't remember who came up with that, but LaMarr never seemed to get ruffled by anything. Just give him the ball every fifth day and stay away from him in the clubhouse for a few hours before each game he started.

I never figured how a man with such tiny fingers could make his pitches move so much. And he was a fast worker, which fielders always love. LaMarr shut down the Royals in a hurry on September 1, and Rudy Law yelled, "Man, you only needed 89 pitches." Lumpy nodded. "Yep, and 86 of them were on the black," he said. That probably was true. The guy walked only 31 batters all through 1983, and four of those were intentional. He could throw a baseball across a dime nine times out of 10. They should have shipped him right to Cooperstown.

LaMarr was a Good Ole Carolina Boy, so we were all sad to hear that he had trouble with drugs later in his career. When he was with the White Sox he was a big reason for our success.

"RICH" SOURCE ON HOYT

> *In the minors, LaMarr Hoyt threw only his sinking fast-ball for strikes. After he came to the White Sox in the 1977 trade that sent shortstop Bucky Dent to the Yankees, the chunky right-hander developed the slider, changeup and pinpoint control that made him the AL's 1983 Cy Young Award winner.*
>
> *"One thing this guy never lacked was confidence," said Paul Richards, the former White Sox manager who scout-ed Hoyt in the minors. "He was a Knoxville reliever then, so I had him throw in the bullpen. He stuck with a full windup. I asked him, 'Why don't you work from a stretch?' He told me, 'No need. I don't have to pitch much with run-ners on.' That attitude made him a winner everywhere."*

IRON FISK, SMOOTH GLOVE

Carlton Fisk had a pretty sly sense of humor, along with his ability. We already knew in '83 that he'd be headed for the Hall of Fame, even though his career lasted 10 more years after that.

The notebooks and cameras crowded into the clubhouse one afternoon, waiting for the victorious Hoyt to emerge from the showers. Fisk strolled by, wrapped in a towel and said, "You have to admit, LaMarr has a lot of stomach—I mean guts." Then he gave them a wink. It was a lot different from the first few months, when Pudge was brooding and wondering if the wheels were coming off.

But he could get through to unhappy pitchers like Dennis Lamp, who kept expecting to get traded. I don't think Fisk was the best catcher I saw in the majors, but he was good. The main thing was that he communicated with the young pitchers, and he could hit. All that noise in the media about Pudge being temperamental didn't bother anybody on the White Sox, except maybe Tony La Russa. What we used to complain about was the way he slowed up games. We'd see him trudge out to the mound with the mask on top of his head, and a three-hour game turned into a four-hour game. He was deliberately slow, I guess to get on the same page with the pitcher. For a high-energy guy like me, it was kind of irritating.

HE FISK RIGHT IN

> South Side fans are always ready to get emotionally involved in baseball, politics or less vital matters.
>
> That's why they are ferociously loyal to their favorite players—Nellie Fox, Minnie Minoso, Jungle Jim Rivera and Ron Kittle, for example—and their favorite mayors, mostly named Daley. But along with those free spirits, combative types also get special dispensation from longtime White Sox rooters. That's why they sided with Carlton Fisk during his running feuds with Sox manager Tony La Russa, Sox chairman Jerry Reinsdorf and other targets of the outspoken catcher's ire. When Fisk and La Russa clashed in 1983, Pudge's version of the dispute drew cheers, while jeers greeted the manager in Comiskey Park.

"They were attacking my roots and they had a fight on their hands," Fisk said. "I was challenged and I had to spit it back. I refused to let people step on my face, so I could be at peace with myself."

HARK THE HAROLD

Even though Harold Baines didn't make lots of noise in the clubhouse, nobody could overlook him.

Harold let his bat do the talking. He was quiet and laid back, which might hurt his chances to get into the Hall of Fame, along with falling just 134 short of the magic number—3,000 career hits. When I played with Harold in the minors, he had trouble catching fly balls. They brought in Jimmy Piersall and Bobby Winkles to hit hundreds of fungoes to him until he got better. Everybody could see the potential, so they were very patient with him. Besides, former Sox owner Bill Veeck made Baines the first draft pick for the White Sox in 1977, passing up future Hall of Famer Paul Molitor to grab him.

That put a high-expectation burden on the youngster, but he eventually justified Veeck's judgment.

"Jumping around and getting all worked up is not my style," said Baines, who returned to newly named U.S. Cellular Field in 2003 as a special assignment instructor for the Sox and served as bench coach in 2004.

THEY WANT NO POT OF IT

After a tough series in Kansas City, Ron Kittle and Harold Baines shared a cab to the airport. Baines was his usual phlegmatic self, although Kittle, frustrated by a weekend of hitting "atom ball" line drives directly into

Royal fielder's gloves, let it all hang out. The cab driver listened patiently, finally breaking into the conversation.

"I got what you guys need," the cabbie said. He pulled down the sun visor on the passenger side to reveal a stash of marijuana cigarettes, rolled and ready to puff away their troubles. He told the astonished players, "A little weed is the secret of hitting. Don't matter if it's on a woman or a baseball." Baines was laughing too hard to speak, but Kittle said, "If that stuff really was the secret of hitting a ball over Willie Wilson's head, I'd buy a truckload."

Neither Baines, the ultimate clean liver, nor Kittle ever used drugs, but from then on, the same driver would pick them up and provide free rides in exchange for tips and autographed baseballs. And if either man needs medical marijuana in Kansas City, they know where to find it.

SOX GET BULLISH

I never saw Greg Luzinski smile during a game. All business, he was a bull of a man, which explains his nickname, but not a bull-headed man. When we got together at his postgame parties, Bull and Jerry Koosman did not rent an extra suite at our road hotels so we could swap stories about what AL cities had the best groupies.

The topic of those group discussions was not always baseball, either. What these smart veterans wanted the whole team to do was kick back, relax and spend some no-sweat time together. It was a good idea, and best of all, it worked.

The White Sox began to put it together on the field, the way we hung together away from the ballpark. Guys had individual players they were closer to, like the friendship I shared with Greg Walker, but there were no cliques. And nobody got left out, even the Latin players like Juan Agosto and Salome Barojas, who seldom got quoted in the papers because they weren't fluent in English.

That kind of "we're all part of this" feeling might have been a bigger contribution to our 1983 division dominance than Luzinski's 32 homers and Koosman's 11 wins, plus a pair of saves in relief. They were both in there pitching for one goal—to get the Sox into the World Series.

When it didn't happen, the young guys felt worse for Kooz than they did for themselves, because they knew he was playing out the string at 40 and this could be his last chance. Those get-togethers were just plain fun, not group therapy or the old guys

Greg "Bull" Luzinski menaces a pitcher. Luzinski was a key for us, not only with his rooftop home runs, but his laid-back leadership off the field.

telling the young guys how things should be done. Whatever it was, the results soon showed up in the AL West standings. Everybody—well, almost everybody—on the White Sox that year—from the manager and coaches to Chicken Willie Thompson, our one-of-a-kind clubhouse man, shared in the daily doings and the credit.

A No-Bull Tale

Besides a big bat at the plate, brawny Bull Luzinski occasionally flashed his droll sense of humor in the clubhouse. We all kidded Jerry Dybzinski, our skinny, six-foot-two shortstop, because he was extremely bowlegged from years of riding in off-season rodeo competition.

Luzinski topped us all one day by proclaiming, "If we could find a way to straighten out Dybber's legs, he'd be seven foot six."

It's Not Basebrawl

Humor also was a big part of what kept the Sox loose throughout 1983's ups and downs. Nobody thought losing was funny, least of all me, but we didn't sit around and brood about the close games that got away early in the season. The clubhouse cut-ups were just biding their time, waiting for the right moment to open the bag of tricks and keep things in a constant state of comic relief.

First, Fisk and Luzinski had to solve the slumps that plagued them both for the opening months, and the starting pitchers needed to hone the razor-sharp edge that made them almost unbeatable down the stretch. I provided a lot of the early offense, and my buddy Greg Walker's confidence grew steadily under La Russa's patient handling.

TONY'S TERRIFIC TWOSOME

"We need some bodies who weren't here last year to come through and pick up the slack," La Russa had prescribed in spring training as his formula to replace Steve Kemp, the 1982 rent-a-body left fielder. He had no way of knowing I would provide 35 homers and 100 RBIs in the upcoming season.

Throw in Walker's 10 home runs and 55 RBIs and it's clear why Sox fans finally stopped second-guessing the manager and started applauding his confidence in Swat and Sweet.

But when Walker's average nosedived in spring training, the lanky Georgian braced for another trip back to the bushes. "I've been trying to crush the ball," he confessed. "I know I can hit up here, so I hope they keep me around long enough to prove it." La Russa, a riverboat gambler at times, decided to roll the dice on Walker and got a handsome payoff. He refused to pull the plug on Greg, even though a pair of errors by the jittery first baseman caused the Whose Sox to lose ugly, 5-3, in the season opener at Texas.

A few months later, Walker's ratio of runs batted in to base hits was among the best in both leagues.

"About then, I didn't hear much from the people who told me Greg was a liability to the White Sox and I was a dunce for keeping him on the roster," La Russa said. "A little while ago, they were complaining I was ruining the kid by pushing him too fast."

LET'S NOT MAKE A DEAL

Before the 1983 trading deadline, when the White Sox were bidding for a proven reliever to beef up their bullpen, team president Eddie Einhorn fielded a phone call from the general manager of an American League rival. "This guy wanted to make a deal, and he just happened to have a spare pitcher," Einhorn said with a chuckle. "All he wanted in return was Ron Kittle and Greg Walker."

SUNSHINE SLUGGERS

In their brief honeymoon with Chicago's media and fans after buying the White Sox from Bill Veeck in 1980, principal owners Jerry Reinsdorf and Eddie Einhorn got labeled "The Sunshine Boys," a title lifted from a hit Broadway show.

A few years later, along came "Swat and Sweet"— right-handed mauler Ron Kittle and lefty swinger Greg Walker, a matched set of promising rookies, at least with a bat in their hands. Both good people, they were temperamentally poles apart, but somehow, free-spirited, garrulous Kittle and quiet, intense Walker became permanent pals, as well as productive performers for the 1983 Sox. Greg spent almost all of his playing career in Chicago and was reunited with Kittle when Ron returned to the Sox in 1989. Walker rejoined the Sox organization and became their big-league batting coach in 2003.

BATMAN AND RONNIE

"When our families get together, the people, places and memories we recall are priceless," Walker said of his years with Kittle. "Now we realize that was the time of our lives, whether we went four for four or wore the collar. I

Kitty once how we got along so well. As usual, he told me more than I needed to know. 'Roomie,' he said, 'We just couldn't stay mad at each other more than a few minutes without busting out laughing. You were a farmer, but I was the one that got up at 5 a.m. You were so intense about baseball, but we still had fun. Basically, we were there for each other.'

"I have to admit he was right about all of that."

Tale of the Tape

One time in spring training, Herm Schneider, our official trainer, was too busy treating other injuries to wrap my sore ankle. So Willie Thompson, our unofficial trainer, volunteered for the job. I should have known better.

He taped it so tight my whole leg was turning blue. I had to rip it off or risk gangrene, but the unflappable Thompson said, "Hey, Kitty, if you don't want it done right, don't ask me to help." Willie and I had good times together, including some wrestling matches you won't see on *Smackdown*, but never again did I let him get close to me with a roll of tape in his gigantic hands.

Floyd's Out of Cluck

No wonder the clubhouse clowning kept us in good spirits. Even Floyd Bannister, a left-hander who blamed himself when things didn't go right on the mound, whether it was his fault or not, gradually learned to relax. Banny had terrific stuff, but he became unglued early in the season when his catcher, Carlton Fisk, and the San Diego Chicken delayed the game with some between-innings horseplay for the TV cameras. Instead of chuckling along with the spectators, Bannister started walking the ballpark, and they had to take him out. A few months later, a cannon could have gone off while he was winding up and Floyd still would have thrown a strike. As a remedy for what ails you, winning beats everything, including Viagra.

CLOSE SHAVE FOR CARTER

Marc Hill didn't care who he sprayed with shaving cream. It was all in fun for Booter, the backup catcher and self-appointed morale officer of the White Sox. He was effective in both roles. Booter's offbeat sense of humor couldn't be restrained even when a former president, Jimmy Carter, visited the team. For Ron Kittle, and a lot of other players, alarm bells started ringing.

"In spring training, somebody would yell, 'Kitty, a phone call for you.' Go into the clubhouse, pick up the phone and Zap! I've got an earful of shaving cream," Kittle recalled. "Hill did it to everybody.

"So when Booter came out of the trainer's room and said very politely, 'Mr. President, you have a phone call,' we all thought, 'Oh, no!' Somebody said, 'If he pulls that stunt on the president, the Secret Service will throw us all in jail.' Well, nobody got arrested, but I think Jimmy Carter wound up with shaving cream in his ear."

THE GAG'S ALL HERE

Nobody ever really got Booter. He was too quick for us. Marc used to go to novelty stores and buy those exploding packs of cigarettes. Then he'd sneak around to the smokers' lockers, especially Jim Leyland's, dump a few out of their packs and load a couple of exploding cartridges in the tips. You could get a puff from the loaded one before it blew up in your hand.

Leyland, our third base coach and a terrific human being, was a very nervous man. Between innings, he'd duck into the dugout tunnel, light up, and we'd quiet down to hear the explosion. Hill did the same thing to Jerry Koosman—put it in his pipe. After the bang, you'd hear "God damn it, Booter!" The coaches used to meet in Tony's office before games. It made our day when we heard Leyland yelling through the door, "Go to hell, Hill!" We'd be rolling on the floor, laughing our guts out. It really sounds like a bunch of kids at summer camp, but you know what? It was funny. Kept us from worrying about anything except who his next victim would be.

Hill of an Explosion

The pressure was off and, making mincemeat of our Western Division rivals, we needed three more victories to nail down their first postseason berth in 24 years when the lowly Seattle Mariners came to town in mid-September.

Just to make sure no last-minute jitters would delay the long-awaited champagne shower, Marc Hill victimized fellow prankster Tom Paciorek with a loaded cigarette. The Sox got an even bigger bang out of it on clinching night, September 17, when Booter got his favorite patsy, coach Jim Leyland, one more time. As soon as Leyland touched a match to his smoke, it went up in smoke, accompanied by a gleeful roar from the players. Even manager Tony La Russa let his game face ease into a grin.

"Some tense club, huh?" La Russa growled, enjoying Hill's take-it-easy technique. "We're trying to get this race over with and Booter's trickin' people on the bench. Our guys were laughing so hard, it's a wonder anybody could swing a bat."

I'm taking some swings in spring training with Marc Hill catching. Hill was the ultimate jokester. Not even former President Carter was exempt from his antics.

TONY THE TIGER

Tony La Russa had that kind of mental and physical toughness, too. He went nose to nose with Doug "Red Rooster" Rader, manager of the Texas Rangers and one of baseball's real rough-and-ready guys. And Tony had to be restrained from starting a punchout with Brewers coaches and players during that Milwaukee border war in July. He stuck up for his players and we returned the loyalty—or most of us, anyway. That had a lot to do with the unselfish attitude on the White Sox.

Ballplayers are emotional people, with lots of pride. That leads to an occasional battle of wills between players and players, players and coaches and sometimes players and their manager on the same team. We had our share early, notably the who's-the-boss dispute between catcher Carlton Fisk and manager Tony La Russa, a couple of headstrong dudes. Pitcher Dennis Lamp came to training camp very unhappy because the arbitrator denied his salary bid in the range of Floyd Bannister's $900,000-plus contract.

"My figures key off his salary," Lamp grumbled. "If Floyd gets that, I'm worth at least $750,000. This club doesn't need me. If they won't trade me, I can always play third base."

Lamp Lightens Load

Fortunately for the White Sox, Lamp stayed put, not at third base or at second fiddle, either. His ruffled feelings soothed by self-hypnosis, the chunky right-hander hung around as a spot starter and wound up bolstering the bullpen with a staff-high 15 saves. Besides that, he was one of the greatest all-time mimics I've seen in baseball or show business, keeping us laughing with his dead-ringer imitations. Dennis could not only talk like anybody he wanted to, but he could reproduce the guy's exact same mannerisms. We'd be sitting on the grass, doing our pregame stretching exercises and laughing so hard we'd bust a gut at those antics. Lamp lit up every hitter, every pitcher, even the umpires. He and Kevin Hickey roomed together, and it was a riot to see them get going together.

Kevin's the sort of person who's high on life, just good to have around. He was as grateful to be part of the White Sox as I was. Every day I went to the park looking for something positive to happen, and it usually did. I understand what a strain the constant pressure to perform can be, but after the Sox got rolling in '83, it was almost like going to the circus, at home or on the road. Most of the players felt the same way I did. You get into a situation that good only a couple of times in your life, so if anyone can't enjoy it while it's happening, he's not very bright.

HICK, HICK, HOORAY

Even the veterans enjoyed Hickey, a Chicago South Sider who had just as much fun playing 16-inch softball as he did being in a pennant race. It was a shame he got hurt and had to sit out most of 1983. Hick was never afraid to run out of the bullpen and take the ball, no matter how many runners were on or who was up. If Babe Ruth and Mickey Mantle were batting from opposite sides of the plate at the same time, Kevin would get on the mound and take his chances. He was a competitor, even standing in the dugout runway to puff on a cigarette and making sure Booter Hill wasn't sneaking up on him. Whenever pitching coach Dave Duncan started looking around for a middle reliever, Hickey was the first one to jump up.

"Kevin's our kind of guy," Tony La Russa said. "We don't want to take any chances with his future."

Unfortunately, Hickey couldn't regain his velocity, so he went back to playing hard-nosed softball.

WIMPY FLIPS OUT

Then there was the noisy, thankfully brief revolt staged by Tom Paciorek, one of our three revolving first basemen. Unhappy about sharing playing time with Greg Walker and Mike Squires at first base and occasionally with me in left field, Paciorek took out his ire on Tony La Russa via a "play me or trade me" blast. Wimpy escalated his "nyah, nyah, nyah" tantrum into a personal grudge between himself and the manager. Pretty articulate for a ballplayer, as he proved during a long stretch with Hawk Harrelson in the White Sox TV booth, Tommy let his unhappiness about not being in the daily starting lineup distract from our struggles to get untracked early in the season.

That was unlike the guy who kept the clubhouse mellow with his comedy routines. Paciorek was a team player, but he always got laughs by bellowing, "It's not what you do for the team—it's what you can do for the Wimper." One day he broke us up by sprinkling baby powder on his hair, making it look whiter than it already was. Remember, folks, this is a roomful of mostly overgrown kids, not your average sophisticated audience at a Rush Street comedy club. Wimpy was always telling jokes and he had a good memory for stories and details, so I wasn't surprised when he turned into an entertaining color announcer.

The important thing is that wherever you put Paciorek, he did his job. He was the only .300 hitter on the '83 team, at .307, with a respectable 63 RBIs. So everybody felt better when Tom cooled off, apologized to La Russa and agreed to accept whatever role allotted to him. Later, on reflection, the former University of Houston defensive back, who was a ninth-round draft choice of the Miami Dolphins in 1968, two years before the AFL-NFL merger, has only one regret. It's his "character assassination" of La Russa.

KING KONG KITTLE

Tom Paciorek wasn't the only person impressed with Ron Kittle's strapping physique when he saw the White Sox rookie step from the showers in the White Sox clubhouse. Paciorek, who later became Hawk Harrelson's TV sidekick, better known as "Wimpy" on Sox telecasts, was even more awed by Kittle's prodigious pokes in batting practice and games. He compared his muscular teammate to King Kong, the gigantic gorilla of movie fame.

"The last thing I saw as strong as Kitty was hanging from the Empire State Building with one paw and holding Faye Wray in the other paw," Paciorek said.

Bat-Bashers, Inc.

We all get like that, and if anybody laughs, we just get madder. I've taken bats up the dugout tunnel and demolished them against the wall, turning good wood into toothpicks. I finally figured out that the only thing I hurt by breaking bats was my hands, so I stopped. On the big-league level, the game is such an intense atmosphere that just about everybody I ever played with or against had to go wild and blow off some steam when things kept heading in the wrong direction. Harold Baines somehow stayed above all that.

He was as ferocious a competitor as I was, but I can't remember ever seeing him lose control of his emotions. When pitchers knocked him down, instead of threatening to charge the mound, Harold would step back in and line the next pitch past their ear, into center field.

Our Unsung, but Not Unseen Hero

It was easy to overlook what Willie Thompson did for the White Sox, because he worked behind the scenes. His official job description was clubhouse/equipment manager, but he deserved a more imposing title, maybe Senior VP for Crisis Control.

Nothing happened in the Sox dressing room that Willie couldn't handle. He was the lone exception to every rule of clubhouse etiquette, spoken or unspoken. As such, he was as important to our success as anyone on the field. But overlook Willie Thompson himself?

Not a chance. At maybe 300 pounds, probably more, this man mountain cut an imposing figure.

His nickname, Chicken Willie, was well earned, because he snacked on whole fryers, hot or cold. So was his reputation for doing whatever needed to be done. I saw him hoist fully loaded equipment trunks in and out of trucks like they were toys on a thousand getaway days, although his sense of humor and ability to get along with everybody was his real strength. Happy-go-lucky Willie kept the clubhouse loose, before, during and after every game. In all those years, I never saw him get too upset to take the pressure off by saying something funny. If it weren't for his antics in the minors, I probably would have been too uptight to swing at the ball, let alone hit it.

At Knoxville, the White Sox' AA farm club, I'd come in early to take extra batting practice and Willie already would have every pair of spiked shoes in the clubhouse knotted together. You never heard such a torrent of profanity from guys running around looking for shoelaces to replace the ones they had to cut with a knife.

Willie just laughed, and they cooled off. He and I later decided we got to Knoxville too soon, instead of waiting for Michael Jordan to come along with his luxury bus for road trips. I didn't have a glove without "Willie Kittle" scrawled on it with a marker pen. For the other guys, theirs was labeled "Willie Fisk" or "Willie Walker" or whatever. Everybody loved the guy. With all that kibitzing, we saw how hard he worked. Chicken Willie is one of those exceptional people. He was still your friend when everything you hit went straight into a fielder's glove, the fans were booing and the manager got mad at you for missing a sign.

DOWN AND DIRTY

Dick "Dirt" Tidrow, another veteran reliever, was a valuable clubhouse asset for the White Sox, just like Jerry Koosman. Right-hander Tidrow and lefty Koosman had been through it all in the big time, including playoff pressure. They were unselfish guys, always ready to give younger pitchers a tip or explain the best way to handle any situation. Their real value to the team probably wasn't appreciated until they departed and the Sox couldn't recapture the magic that brought them to the doorstep of the 1983 World Series.

"I know how to pitch, and I keep the ball in the park," Tidrow said of his knack for not serving up game-breaking home run balls to opposing hitters in tense relief situations.

About the only time Dirt was caught with egg on his face all season happened when his four-year-old son, Andrew, wandering around the clubhouse, found a jock strap in an adjoining locker and draped it on his head. "Look, Dad, Ron Kittle's got a gas mask," Andrew said. When the roar of laughter died down, I told Tidrow, "Don't worry, it's a clean one."

DOT HITS THE SPOT

Richard Dotson was the quiet man in our starting rotation. I saw Dot pitch for the Angels' farm team in Idaho, cutting loose about 100 miles an hour. He was just as likely to kill you as throw a strike, because he had no idea where the ball was going.

When Dotson got to the White Sox, he also had a terrific changeup, but LaMarr Hoyt completely overshadowed him. Hoyt was an intriguing story ever since the 1979 trade that brought him to Chicago, along with Oscar Gamble. The Yankees really wanted Bucky Dent from the White Sox, so they figured Hoyt was a throw-in on the deal. The California Angels thought the same thing about Dotson, when they dealt him to the Sox in 1977 for Brian Downing, a durable clutch hitter.

Angels scout Del Rice, who caught such winners as Howie Pollet, Vinegar Bend Mizell and Warren Spahn in his long career, was horrified when Dotson got away. Another respected ivory hunter, the Reds' Ray Shore, also couldn't believe it.

"Throw-in?" Shore said. "This kid can be the next Tom Seaver."

Sadly, that's not how it worked out. Although Seaver and Dotson later were Sox teammates, 1983 was Dot's lone big season. The fireballing right-hander was 22-7 then, but arm problems soon doused the flame in his high hard one. "Don Drysdale got my mechanics straightened out," Dotson said of the Sox broadcaster, who once teamed with the Dodgers' Sandy Koufax to form baseball's most feared 1-2 pitching punch. "We knew things would come around on that '83 team, but I admit we never dreamed lightning would strike everybody at the same time."

Good Cast, Heck of a Plot

Our coaches seldom get the credit they deserved. Jim Leyland (third base coach), Dave Duncan (pitching coach), Charley Lau (hitting instructor), Eddie Brinkman (fielding) and Davey Nelson (baserunning, first base coach) made up the best staff I've ever been around. Those guys all had different personalities that blended well. And let's not forget Art Kusnyer, the bullpen coach.

Everybody called him "Cave," because he was a throwback to the cavemen, a real character, if I ever saw one. Cave was a tough guy and a great storyteller, even though you couldn't repeat too many of his tales in mixed company. The first thing

Artie will tell you is that he caught one of Nolan Ryan's seven no-hit games.

A Fast Exit

Art Kusnyer, serving his second term as the bullpen coach for the White Sox, is still telling stories and helping young players to find their way around the American League. He also lightens the mood by recalling his last at-bat in the minors, closing out a playing career that spanned 14 seasons and 13 teams, including one hit in 10 trips for the 1970 White Sox.

"I came up to bat for Iowa, watching a huge relief pitcher named Dave Stephan lumber in from the bullpen, with mustard on his jersey," Kusnyer said. "He picked up the rosin bag and tore it in half. The catcher was Bruce Kimm, who became the Cubs manager in 2002 after Don Baylor got fired.

"I told Bruce, 'Don't throw me any curves.' He said 'Nothing to worry about, Cave. He ain't got one.' So I struck out on three straight fastballs. The slowest one was 130 miles an hour."

Brain Trust Bonanza

I can't imagine a group of people with so much specialized knowledge getting together ever again as coaches for one team. I was very fortunate to come to the White Sox with a supportive bunch like this, from Tony La Russa to Willie Thompson, the man who ran the show in the clubhouse just as intensely as Tony in the dugout.

These were baseball lifers. They discarded their egos along with their street clothes when it was time to put on a uniform and go to work. The players were not overshadowed by them,

Wearing the home white uniform at Comiskey Park was always a pleasure.

and they stuck together without back-stabbing each other or brown-nosing the front office. If a player was at fault, the coaches would jump in and deflect the blame to themselves. I look back on it now and realize I considered all of those guys more as my friends then as my bosses. The 1983 Sox were a team with more than 25 bodies on the roster.

LEYLAND'S THE MAN

Jimmy Leyland was the only one of those coaches who went on to be a big-league manager. He got the most out of lineups with lots less talent than the White Sox when he took over in Pittsburgh and elsewhere. I believe Duncan, Brinkman and Nelson could have been winning skippers, too, but those jobs seem to wind up with the same Good Ole Boys on the revolving door list that keeps replacing each other.

It is true that many outstanding coaches lack a manager's personality.

I mean, you practically have to be a father, mother, brother, friend, teacher, motivator and psychologist for a dugout full of temperamental personalities. And no matter what the manager wants them to do, they all want it done their way. We had our share of those problems on the White Sox, and Tony's emotional nature might not have been able to solve them without his coaches backing him all the way. They had a knack for preventing the pot from boiling over.

BP OR NOT BP?

We had a tremendous coaching staff, but Leyland and Brinkman, the guys who threw batting practice to Harold Baines, Greg Walker and me, were not the best pitchers in the world. Even when Leyland's pitches sailed over my head, I'd swing at everything or catch the ball bare-handed and toss it back to him.

The main thing was, we had fun with each other. When writers asked me the toughest pitcher I faced, I'd say, "Jimmy Leyland." He got a big kick out of that. Leyland never failed to point out that his BP group led the AL in RBI with a total of 254—100 for me, 99 for Baines and 55 for Walker—only he called them "rib-eyes." Jimmy used to say "Thanks to me, those three guys gave the White Sox more rib-eyes than Ponderosa Steak House."

Basically, my hitting routine was changing bats a lot. If the one I used in BP didn't work, I figured it wouldn't know where to find a pitch during the game. I always thought good batting practice set up a good game for me. Even with all the kidding, Leyland and Brinkman did a lot to help.

The Book on .300

Charley Lau was a good hitting teacher but he didn't change my style. His video, "The Art of Hitting .300" had a picture of me on the front in my favorite pose—at the plate, bat cocked, eyes on the pitcher.

His fundamentals made sense to me: Good balance, hands up high, finish the swing high, head on the ball. I always let go of the bat with one hand at the end of my swing, even in Little League. That's what Charley tried to reinforce when he started working with me as the White Sox batting instructor. Mainly, I never wanted to step out of the batting cage until I got a couple of good swings. I still tell kids, "Take a positive attitude out of practice and visualize that result in the game." I get pumped up about convincing them to stay within their own talent.

Believe it or not, the biggest curse I had to deal with was having power. I couldn't worry about singles.

My swing was tuned to gap-to-gap line drives, depending on where the pitch came in. My home runs mostly were liners, although the seven roofers I hit at old Comiskey Park all had to get up in the air fast.

I bounced a couple more near-misses off the upper-deck facade. Those long ones were on mistakes by the pitcher, pretty much low and out over the plate so I could extend my arms, get under the ball and elevate it in a hurry. I didn't drive many pitches above my chest level. If my neck and back felt good that day, what I wanted to do was knock the pitcher off the mound with every swing.

SADNESS AMID SUCCESS

Despite becoming the winningest team in either league, a shadow that could not be lifted by success and togetherness hung over the 1983 season. My Dad, James "Slim" Kittle, along with White Sox coaches Charley Lau and Loren Babe, had been stricken with cancer. Within a few years, all three men died of the disease. My father was undergoing treatment, but he came to Comiskey Park for some home games, often sitting with Roland Hemond, the Sox general manager and a great and supportive friend of the Kittle family.

Almost everybody on the roster had been tutored and befriended by Lau and Babe, who knew how hard life could be for young players in the minor leagues, many away from home for the first time in their lives.

Nobody took Babe's death in 1984 harder than manager Tony La Russa. Babe had been the manager in Denver, then a Sox farm affiliate, in 1975, and LaRussa played four positions for that team, making a lasting impression with his will to win. It was Babe's recommendation that got Tony his first manageri-al job with class AA Knoxville, in 1978. Just one year later, ex-Cub shortstop Don Kessinger got fired as the White Sox manager, turning over the reins to the untested, virtually unknown, La Russa.

A Noble Gift

Loren Babe, who played briefly in the majors with the Yankees and Philadelphia A's before spending more than three decades as a minor-league coach and manager, was a few months short of eligibility for baseball's pension and medical benefits plan. When hitting instructor Charley Lau heard that Babe had lung cancer, he stepped down as a White Sox coach, so Babe could be added to the roster long enough to qualify for pension rights. "Don't make a big deal out of this," insisted Lau, who always dodged the spotlight.

The tragic irony was that Lau soon underwent surgery for colon cancer. He insisted on rejoining the Sox to work with young hitters until the fatal illness weakened him. "I'll never be able to repay Charley," Babe said. "It just about killed me when I heard he had cancer, too."

Law-breaker on Base

Rudy Law had little respect for the law when it came to stealing bases. That's what made him such an effective leadoff man for the White Sox. We called him "Rudy D," maybe because he was so daring when it came to taking big leads, rattling opposing pitchers and running whenever he got a jump. His 77 stolen bases in 1983 still is the all-time Sox record.

Chances are it will stand for a long time, since baseball's become more and more of a longball, big-inning game and less of a get 'em on, get 'em over, get 'em in affair. We could play it both ways in '83, because Julio Cruz also was a base-stealing threat and La Russa liked to run on pitchers who didn't have strong pickoff moves. Believe it or not, I stole eight bases in 11 attempts that season.

I first met Rudy when we were both in the Dodgers' organization. It turned out to be a break to get away from them, although neither of us thought so at the time. I figured my career might be over almost before it started when the Dodgers released me. And Rudy's confidence really took a beating from the way they treated him. He learned to relax and have fun when he came to the White Sox in a 1982 trade that was a real steal, pun intended. We sure took advantage of his speed.

Actually, Rudy didn't become our starting center fielder until veteran Ron LeFlore got conked on the head with a fly ball, but baseball is full of such strange twists, just like life. It took a few breaks for me to escape the discard pile and make the big leap from a never-was with the Dodgers to the American League's 1983 Rookie of the Year.

Rudy had to get here the hard way, too, so we bonded well. Tommy Lasorda, the fast-talking LA manager, thought I ate too much at the Dodgers' rookie camp, and he sent Law back to the minors one too many times.

"Whenever I made a mistake, Lasorda dumped on me," Law recalled. "He wouldn't embarrass the veterans, but I got loud-talked in front of other people. I was glad to get out of there."

Law credited his wife, Evelyn, with rebuilding his confidence. She even pitched a cotton ball to him, helping the lefty batter improve his timing on changeups. The effectiveness of the Lawman and his deputy was confirmed by Jim Russo, the Baltimore superscout whose book on the White Sox enabled the Orioles to read between the lines in our playoff showdown for the 1983 AL pennant.

"You don't need a Hall of Fame center fielder to be a contender," Russo reported. "Law's speed and ability to get on base make him superior to others with equal defensive ability."

Law's a Lawn Hog

> *When the White Sox of 1983 came back to Chicago to celebrate the 20th anniversary of their Western Division championship season, tall tales were flying around U.S. Cellular Field much like baseballs used to soar into the stands at Comiskey Park, just across the street.*
>
> *In this get-together, Ron Kittle agreed, they stuck by the unwritten rule that home runs grow 100 feet in length with each passing year.*
>
> *Rudy Law greeted Kittle with this remark: "You and Baines tired me out. I had to play left-center for you, right-center for Harold Baines and center for me." Baines had a quick comeback: "Rudy D, that's what center fielders are for."*

"Do-Be" Law

They put the player of the game on a radio show in 1983, and that's how Rudy got another nickname—"Do-be." Asked why he didn't drink water before games to avoid getting dehydrated, Law replied, "I run the bases so much, I do be tired when I drink a lot."

Whatever Rudy was doing that year, it paid off. Artie Kusnyer, our bullpen coach and one-liner specialist, summed it up by saying, "Right now, Rudy's confidence is higher than a giraffe's entrails."

Law and Order at Third

The White Sox looked everywhere to find a quality third baseman, floating more trade rumors early in 1983 than the

New York Stock Exchange. They already had the right one, only Vance Law was so quiet and easygoing that he got overlooked.

Fortunately, when hot deals for Buddy Bell, John Castino, or Lance Parrish came undone, the situation really was Law and orderly. Vance Law came over from Pittsburgh in a 1982 trade. Law, an unassuming, squeaky-clean Mormon, was first rate at third base. He had a cannon for an arm, probably inherited from his father, Vern Law, a long-time pitcher for the Pirates. Not a flashy fielder, Vance could knock down grounders, scramble for the ball and throw out all but the fastest runners.

Lorenzo Gray tried to take the starting job away from him, but Vance had that no-nonsense determination to win it back. He wanted to prove that his ability, not the family name, earned playing time. He did, although there were a lot of Law family members around when we played the Pirates in spring training. Vance was a teetotaler, like the rest of them, somehow dodging the rivers of champagne flowing through the clubhouse the night we clinched the division title.

"I've never tasted alcohol, but there was so much flying around, I must have soaked up some through my pores," he said with a sheepish grin. "I still feel a little giddy."

Both Laws on the White Sox, Rudy and Vance, were good people from high-class families. It's customary to say that about every ex-teammate, of course, but in all honesty, there was not one man on this team I disliked or had squabbles with. It's another reason why that year stands out. Vance wore glasses, like me, so the fans got us confused. "Hey, Kittle!" they'd yell at him. Then they'd ask him how such a slender guy could hit those long home runs. I hope he didn't give away my secrets.

No Shortstop Shortage

The Yankees had their Scooter, a very classy little guy named Phil Rizzuto, in the broadcast booth for years after his long

reign as their shortstop. We had our own version at short in
Scotty Fletcher. He was such a hustler, always on the move, that
we called him Scooter. He was a hard worker, a good kid. He
battled Jerry Dybzinski all season for the starting job, so Tony
could play "who's hot, who's not" with them.

Scott worked so hard that he wore himself out, because he
was not a Cal Ripken Jr., Robin Yount-type power shortstop.
He had a football mentality though, from playing in college at
Akron, where his father coached the Zips.

Fletcher came from the Cubs in yet another front-office bur-
glary by Roland Hemond. The Sox general manager palmed off
Steve Trout and Warren Brusstar to the Cubs in exchange for
Fletcher, Dick Tidrow, Pat Tabler and Randy Martz. Trout, a
somewhat eccentric left-hander in the classic mold of Ring
Lardner's "You Know Me, Al," did contribute heavily to Dallas
Green's North Side "New Tradition," helping the Cubs to end
their 39-year postseason drought in 1984. But Trout was feuding with Tony La Russa and pitching badly for the Sox, so he
had to go somewhere. Both Fletcher and Tidrow paid immediate dividends in their new home.

It didn't seem that way at first, with Fletcher committing
nine of the 20 errors racked up by the butterfingered Sox in
their first 20 games. Temporarily, Jerry Dybzinski, a six-foot-
two, bow-legged refugee from the Cleveland Indians, took over
at short. Fletcher soon patched the hole in his glove, and when
second baseman Julio Cruz came over from Seattle on June 15
in a swap for Tony Bernazard, The Juice and The Scooter
promptly teamed up to become one of the AL's best double-play
combinations. That was cool, especially with Sox fans who happened to be teenage girls. They swooned over Fletcher's boyish
handsomeness, just like young ladies in Wrigley Field did at the
sight of Cubs second baseman Ryne Sandberg.

But as Yankees catcher Yogi Berra, not exactly a *GQ* poster
boy, observed, "You don't hit a baseball with your face." Fletcher
had to demonstrate to his teammates that he was willing to get

his uniform dirty, but the eager-beaver newcomer's hyperactive intensity soon cleared that hurdle.

"Harold Baines and I don't show our emotion, but Scotty does," Greg Luzinski noted approvingly. "A winning club needs that blend of temperaments."

DYBBER DOES THE JOB

It's a real shame that Jerry Dybzinski's career with the White Sox all came down to one mistake on the basepaths. At least, that's the way Sox fans look at it. They'll never forget or forgive him for getting caught off second base in the final game of our playoff with the Orioles. That tough-luck play shouldn't erase the memory of a terrific season, and the Dybber contributed his share. He made one big out, but the rest of us had 29 more outs to score some runs that day, and we didn't get it done. When something bad happens, no matter how good everything else went up to that, there always has to be a scapegoat. They're still looking to pin the blame on somebody for starting the Great Chicago Fire back in 1871.

It's a good thing Jerry had the mental makeup to handle all the criticism he got. It started way before the playoffs, as soon as the Sox traded a young prospect, Pat Tabler, to the Indians for Dybzinski on April Fool's Day. The Dybber showed up with a "fringe player, can't hit, stone hands" label pinned on him by the Cleveland writers.

"I didn't read the rips on me," Dybzinski said. "If I had, it wouldn't change my attitude or stop me from trying to help the White Sox. People are always being prejudged. I've been called 'Cowboy' and a lot worse, because I'm bow-legged. The only way I'd notice my legs was if I stood in front of a mirror."

Fortunately for the rest of the team, Dybber didn't waste much time posing. He pitched in wherever needed, and the stat that showed nine of his 16 runs batted in coming with two outs proved more about his value than getting caught off base one time. Jerry Koosman, the clubhouse elder statesman, summed it up for everybody when he said, "Jerry got us over that early-season hump."

A team player, he also had an outstanding sense of humor. I could sit and listen to the comedy routines between Dybber, Dennis Lamp and Art Kusnyer for days. Put the three of them together and you'd get some hysterical conversation. Dybzinski perfected the dead-fish handshake. He'd shake with you, pull his hand away and it would feel like a limp sardine slipping out of your hand. When I saw him for the first time in years at the '83 team reunion, he pulled that handshake on me and I had to bust out laughing again, just like always.

I tell Sox fans the same thing when they bring up Dybber's playoff boo-boo. It's just as dumb to blame him for the White Sox not getting into the 1983 World Series as it is to blame Steve Bartman (the notorious ball-deflecting fan in Game 6 of the NL Championship Series) for the Cubs not getting into the 2003 World Series. Two heartbreaking plays for Chicago in two crucial games, 20 years apart. My point is, you can't dwell on any one play, because hundreds of little things led up to those situations.

ROLES LET SOX ROLL

Just ask Jerry Koosman, who helped pitch the Cubs out of the 1969 NL playoffs and played a big part in getting the White Sox into the 1983 AL playoffs. He was one of several guys who accepted their roles, did their parts and let the everyday players—including me—take most of the bows. Not enough credit went to Kooz, Mike Squires, the slick-fielding first baseman, pinch hitter deluxe Jerry Hairston, plus relievers Juan Agosto and Dirt Tidrow.

Remember, we lost Jim Kern, projected as a starter, in the second game of the season. I was playing left field at Texas that night, and I heard Kern scream with pain when he threw a pitch in the first inning that tore the tendons away from his right elbow. We all ran in and stood around the mound while trainer Herm Schneider did what he could to help Kern, but surgery couldn't repair the damage, and the veteran's career was over.

Then reliable lefty reliever Kevin Hickey went down with a shoulder injury, so we were leading only the Aspirin League for a while. That's when Koosman and Tidrow proved their worth, running an unofficial anti-panic clinic in the clubhouse. Those crafty old warhorses steadied everybody's nerves, kept our fingers from groping for the panic button and passed on useful tips to the young pitchers.

Kooz even talked hitting with me, advising what to expect from various AL pitchers in certain situations.

HE KNOWS THE O'S

Like Tidrow, Koosman played old-fashioned, hard-core baseball. He wasn't afraid to drill an opposing hitter with a pitch when the other team had been coming too close with brushbacks. They were students of the game, caring about what was happening at every position on the field. Wily, vocal guys, Dirt and Kooz never hesitated to say what they thought needed to be said, including positioning the fielders when they wanted to work a certain way on a batter.

A few years ago, Koosman stayed at my house in Indiana while he recuperated from open-heart surgery. We watched one of those TV classic shows when he pitched for the New York Mets against Baltimore in the 1969 World Series. Jerry sat on my couch and recreated, pitch by pitch, what he threw to the Orioles. He won some big games for the Mets and 14 years later, there he was in Chicago, doing the same thing for the White Sox.

I know Cub fans don't have fond memories of Koosman, a big reason why their team fell out of first place in 1969, ruining the best chance Ron Santo, Ernie Banks, Billy Williams and all of those guys had to play in the World Series. I asked him if the Mets felt like villains for beating out those lovable Cubs, the team most of the country seemed to be rooting for.

"To tell the truth, Kitty, our guys never thought much about the Cubs," Kooz told me. "They were on top until August, but once we got rolling, we knew nobody could beat us."

I remember that season and how depressed the fans got, crying about the way the Cubs blew it. Well, they really didn't, because the Mets played better baseball down the stretch. That's how the White Sox won their division in 1983, and Koosman did a lot more to get us there than just win 11 games. He had the mental toughness to concentrate on his job and leave the hand-wringing to others.

JUICE IN TIME

The final piece of the puzzle was supplied by the arrival of Julio "Juice" Cruz in June to camp out at second base. Live-wire Cruz proved an immediate hit with the fans, especially when he unveiled his crowd-pleasing specialty, the Juice Jump—a standing leap from the dugout to the top of the steps leading to the field. Along with his bubbly personality, it didn't hurt a bit that Cruz could swing the bat, steal a base and blend with another bundle of nervous energy, shortstop Scott Fletcher, to play good D around the keystone sack. A lucrative new contract awaited him in Chicago, but he shrugged off the speculation about big bucks by chirping, "Everybody wants to have a good year so they'll make more money. They forget how to have fun."

Not on the White Sox, we hadn't—at least in 1983. That was the year that was for all of us, and we made the most of it, including Cruz. His flashy defense deflected criticism when he started off in a one-for-17 slump, although things soon fell into place for him, just as it had for everybody else. After calling his shot—at least, according to reliever Salome Barojas—on a game-breaking homer in Kansas City, the newcomer from Seattle told the media, "Kingdome homers don't count. This was my first one outdoors all year."

I respectfully disagreed, recalling the one I launched off Matt Young of the Mariners, almost to the Dome's back wall, upstairs in left-center. Nobody had hit one up there before, but when Mark McGwire homered in almost the same spot, the Mariners painted the seat where his landed. Anyway, Juice gave us all a boost when he came on board. He was a big-time, high-energy second baseman, quite a change from the man he replaced, Tony Bernazard, who was basically going through the motions. Cruz could turn the double play, but what he did best was put some life in the lineup. Julio was always shaking and twitching.

The picture of him jumping on home plate on September 17 with the run that clinched the division title for the Sox sort of summed up the whole season. As a team, we stomped on everybody down the stretch.

NA, NA NOW, NANCY

Almost everybody who went to Comiskey Park, from the 1970s right up to today, where the new stadium, right across 35th Street, has been renamed U.S. Cellular Field, is a fan of organist Nancy Faust—including me.

She could belt out a tune from Scott Joplin's ragtime beat all the way to the latest heavy metal, matching the mood of the spectators or the rythm of the game with equal ease. Her knack of greeting each Sox player's arrival at the plate with a few notes from the signature song she selected for him was pure entertainment. Even now, fans with long memories hum a few bars from "Gary, Indiana" when I take my family to a restaurant and we walk past their tables.

Thanks, Nancy. The kind of good-natured fun she put to music was much more family oriented than Harry Caray's raucous bellow: "Ah, ya can't beat fun at the old ball park."

But the one thing Nancy's admirers and Harry's fanatics always could agree on was her masterpiece.

When she started saluting departing opponents' pitchers and celebrating Sox victories with "Na-Na-Na-Na, Hey, Heyee, Goodbye!", the whole place joined in. Pretty soon the city of Chicago and sometimes it seemed the rest of the country was swaying to Nancy's beat. Copycats from all over still try to imitate her, but just like the 1983 White Sox, she's a one of a kind.

FAUST OR SLOW, SHE'S A HIT

Nancy Faust sent White Sox fans home humming, win or lose. The long-time ballpark organist had these melodic greetings for players when they came to bat:

Rudy Law: "I Fought the Law and the Law Won" or the famous dum-da-dum-dum theme from "Dragnet."

Carlton Fisk: For some reason, his was "Duke of Earl." I don't know why.

Greg Luzinski: A polka, maybe "The Pennsylvania Polka" for his years with the Phillies.

Ron Kittle: "Doo Ron, Ron, Ron" or "Gary, Indiana."

Greg Walker: "Walk Like a Man", "I Walk the Line," or "I'm Walkin' the Floor Over You."

Harold Baines: "He's So Shy" or the Haines underwear jingle, 'cause it rhymes with Baines.

Scott Fletcher: Something with bagpipes or "Me and God are Watching Scotty Grow."

Vance Law: Any theme from TV shows like LA Law.

Tom Paciorek: "He had fun imitating Lawrence Welk, so I played champagne music for him."

Richard Dotson: "The theme from Datsun auto commercials."

Floyd Bannister: "Stairway to Heaven."

Dennis Lamp: "You Light Up My Life."

"And I remember the first time the fans went wild when I played 'Na, Na, Hey, Hey, Goodbye' quite well," Faust said. "It was 1977, the year of the South Side Hit Men and the White Sox were in a race for first place with Kansas City. A Royals pitcher was taken out of the game, and the Bill Veeck-era crowd was so pumped up that night, they responded to anything I played. I had used it before then, between innings and so on, but never got that kind of reaction. After the game, people kept asking, 'What was the song you played that got everybody so excited?' I didn't even know the proper name then. I thought it was 'Sha Na, Na, Goodbye.' Right away, the tune got so popular at other ballparks that later in the year, I received a gold record of it from Mercury. There was so much demand that they re-released the original recording from 'Steam,' the group that made it."

THEY'RE IN TUNE

Nancy Faust is such a neat lady. She still does her homework at U.S. Cellular Field, just like she did at Comiskey Park, so she knows what the players and most of the fans want to hear. When things are going good, the music makes it more fun, but if your luck turns sour, everything begins to affect you. Nancy's a fan, as well as a really good organist, and a few "Let's go, Sox" notes from her could help lighten the mood, perk up the crowd and get them back into the game. She loves animals, so when I heard she lived on a farm with room for "varmints," as she called them, I found a baby chick and gave it to her. She raised it as a pet, not for the lunch menu at KFC.

NOT A POULTRY GESTURE

> *More than two decades later, Nancy Faust still appreciates Ron Kittle's surprise gift of a just-hatched hen. "He walked up to me, said, 'This is the new Nancy F.' and handed me this cute little chick," she recalled.*
>
> *"Ron was the same way with the fans. I never saw him walk past a kid without signing a cap or a scorecard. They crowded around his car so much after games, he couldn't get away for an hour or so. Finally, he had to stop parking in the players' lot."*

THE RUBBER CHICKEN CIRCUIT

White Sox fans liked Nancy and they seemed to like me too, so we wound up going to all kinds of off-season gatherings together. No doubt, her organ music was easier on the ears than my stories, but the people had a good time. Most of me also enjoyed those Hot Stove League events—everything except my digestive tract.

The parasite I picked up in Mexico, and still can't get rid of, kicked up at that steady diet of chicken, which began to taste like rubber after a while. It didn't take me long to figure out why those postseason tours were known as the rubber chicken circuit.

A SLAM DUNC FOR TONY

Another strong link in our success was the way Tony and his pitching coach, Dave Duncan, worked together, thought alike and didn't hang their players out to dry when things went wrong. Wherever La Russa's gone as a manager, Duncan has been with him.

Along with the rest of the position players on the 1983 White Sox, I respected Dunc, and the pitchers had all kinds of rapport with him, not just about the mechanics of their release points. He related to them and he understood the philosophy of pitching, so it was a vote of confidence when he went to the mound and checked them out in a tight spot. They learned to expect a word of encouragement from Duncan instead of a warning that they'd get the hook if they made a mistake. You could see his belief in them building their own confidence. He got the most out of a bullpen that wasn't loaded with talent, but our starting pitchers were so overpowering down the stretch, they didn't need much help.

If you played for Tony La Russa, you played old-school baseball or you sat on the bench. He was a firm believer in protecting his men, so if anybody threw at us, we would retaliate on their best hitter, not at some humpty-dumpty. You won't find that written down in a manager's handbook, but it's his philosophy. LaMarr Hoyt was told to go after a guy, threw at him three or four times and still couldn't plunk him. So Tony sent Duncan out to the mound to tell LaMarr, "Get it done or it'll cost you some money."

MINING DIAMOND GEMS

La Russa stands by his team and he cares about the players' character, not just their ability. You could tell he was an outstanding manager by the coaching staff he put together on the '83 Sox. When they're learning how to manage, sharp ex-players like Tony run across savvy guys in the minors and start collecting them in their head to hire when the big-league job comes along.

The intensity of his coaches reflected Tony's personality. I remember asking baserunning coach Davey Nelson and Jim Leyland, our third-base coach, what my steal sign was. Jimmy didn't bat an eye. "When I jump up in the coaching box and don't come down, that's when you can steal," he said. But Davey knew how to run the bases in his playing days, and he showed us various pitchers' moves, how much of a lead you could take on them, very useful stuff.

Everybody studied hitting, but nobody took it as far as our coach, Charley Lau. He had George Brett on the brink of batting .400 one year (.390 in 1980) and made Reggie Jackson better for both average and homers. When you produce results like that, it puts you on a different level.

That White Sox staff was very close, like a fist with all the fingers backing each other. Charley, a very quiet man, knew he was dying of cancer while the White Sox were turning his teaching into base hits. He'd sit with us on the plane, sip a white wine and talk hitting. He stressed situation hitting, especially making contact to score a runner from third base with less than two out. This man taught me to be positive with every swing I took, but when you're a rookie, it's almost like you don't qualify to talk to the coaches. Just do your job and shut up.

Leyland, they nicknamed "Humperdinck" because he used to dress up and imitate the singer. We had a bunch of characters, but Jimmy had been around baseball a long time, so he knew how to play it, coach it and eventually manage it. A dedicated workaholic, like me, he used to wear me out hitting grounders and fungoes in my direction every day. If a guy blundered on the bases, he took the heat. I'd call Leyland the final piece of the puzzle that made the coaching staff fit together. And he was a terrific traffic cop, with an instinct for sending runners home or holding them up.

HEMOND'S THE HE-MAN

So our South Side cast and crew was ready to put on a hit show that summer. First, somebody had to assemble them all, assigning starring roles to some and bit parts to others. That man, I have absolutely no doubt, was Roland Hemond, general manager of the White Sox.

Roland was instructed by Jerry Reinsdorf and Eddie Einhorn, the bigfoots in the club's executive suite, to assemble a winning team, and that's what he did. Baseball's bottom line and top priority—win or move on—is the same in the front office as it is on the field. And the pressure is just as intense, even though the sound of fans booing the failure to pull off a blockbuster trade is more muffled in the GM's office than it is in the ballpark when somebody strikes out with the bases loaded. But even hard-core fans eventually start voting with their wallets when the home team sinks like the Titanic in the standings. And the testimony of turnstiles rusting while cobwebs sprout on empty seats and the media opens fire makes the loudest noise of all. That sound is sure to be accompanied by roars of rage from the owners' luxury box.

Hemond understands all of that. He's been around the game longer than any except the hardiest of baseball lifers. Unlike some of them, Roland's respected not only for his encyclopedic knowledge, but for his blend of class and character. Right from the start in spring training, he was there to encourage me and the rest of the young players. We talked often, and he was so upbeat that you couldn't help feeling more confident. Every rookie wants to get it done right now, but Hemond counseled patience. That rubbed off on the 1983 White Sox. And nobody enjoyed it more when the new guys, including Greg Walker and me, proved we could contribute.

VEECK AS IN HECK (OF A GUY)

Bill Veeck was the man who brought excitement back to baseball on the South Side of Chicago. Since the Go-Go White Sox of the 1950s turned on the town with their daring, wide-open style, personified by Nellie Fox, Minnie Minoso and Billy Pierce, things slid into a slow decline. Veeck turned the lights on again, electrifying both the scoreboard and the fans with his brand of showmanship. His Sox didn't win any pennants after 1959, but they won the hearts of enough Chicagoans to keep the franchise from going elsewhere.

That would have been a loss to me personally, to thousands of other fans and to the city itself. Instead, the priceless memories and the long tradition of an American League charter franchise were saved for better days and new generations of White Sox boosters. By the way, it preserved Comiskey Park as the setting for a hopeful rookie to make the big time in 1983. That was a big lug named Ron Kittle, and as far as I'm concerned, there was no greater city and no better ballpark for all those good times to happen to me. I'm taking nothing away from Jerry Reinsdorf by saying this. Jerry, Eddie Einhorn and their fellow Sox owners deserve a lot of credit for rebuilding the franchise and making their team AL contenders again. Above all, those guys kept the Chicago White Sox where they belong—in Chicago. They're not playing in Comiskey Park anymore, but the good news is that U.S. Cellular Field is just across the street on the South Side, not somewhere across the country.

But Bill Veeck still holds a special place in the hearts of White Sox fans. That goes for me, as well. He brought a sense of adventure to the ballpark, because the fans never knew what stunt or giveaway or new twist Veeck would add to the game. I remember Ed Barrow, one of those old-time Yankees' general managers, saying, "The only thing we have to sell is baseball." Bill had more to sell along with the game, especially fun.

Of course, I can't forget that Veeck gave me the second chance I needed to make my dream of playing in the big leagues come true. After I hit a dozen or so pitches into the Comiskey Park seats during a 1978 tryout, the then-White Sox owner ordered Roland Hemond not to let me get away without signing a minor-league contract. That was the start of something big for me, for my Northwest Indiana friends and fans and for the Sox, as well. Veeck loved to roll the dice on things his fellow owners regarded as lost causes. I'm glad I was able to make his bet on me a winning one.

HOME "RON" FOR SOX

"I'm pleased to see my baseball people's faith in Ron Kittle created a lot of excitement for White Sox fans this season," Bill Veeck said while the Sox turned the AL West into a one-horse race. "He's the logical choice for (1983) Rookie of the Year in the American League, but as we all know, logic doesn't always prevail in these matters. Even so, a rookie with Kittle's kind of power is hard to find."

Veeck shrugged off Kittle's league-leading strikeout total with his customary wry humor. "Babe Ruth struck out a few times, didn't he?" the master showman chuckled. "He's turned out to be a better defensive outfielder than people expected, but that's strictly a bonus. People are paying their money to see Kittle and Greg Luzinski hit baseballs out of sight and over the roof."

7

JUST CALL HIM BABE ROOF

Kittle's Classic Clouts

While it lasted, I played every game to win and every one of my 176 career homers was a pleasure, especially the 65 I hit in Comiskey Park while a member of the White Sox. The ones the fans still stop me to talk about are the seven rooftop home runs I launched at Comiskey. Some of them even recall the one that just missed, slamming into the facade above the left-field upper deck. That's a good way to start an autograph request, especially if a fan approaches me with a youngster in tow. I like to tell kids they can swing for the fences, too, and watch their eyes light up in anticipation. There's no way to duplicate that sort of thrill. It's like giving Sox fans a reward for their loyalty and something to talk about with their buddies.

Nobody gets that excited about singles, I remember when I was a wide-eyed kid, reading about the way Babe Ruth took that all-or-nothing cut on every pitch. "I could have batted .600 every season, but I would have had to hit them singles," the Bambino said. Well, I went for opposite-field line drives when the situation dictated, but the Babe's go-for-broke gusto was much more appealing to me and to most fans.

I went for the opposite field when the situation dictated, but I preferred to swing hard for the fences.

Not to mention a lot more fun. But it took a certain kind of pitch, with the pitcher supplying some of the power, to lift a ball onto Comiskey's roof. It was 70 feet high, so they calculated a baseball must be driven at least 475 feet, from impact with the bat to landing, to get there.

I didn't realize that pitch from Oakland's Chris Codoroli on September 6, 1983, was gone for good until I got all the way around the bases and the fans wouldn't stop screaming. To get everybody's attention like that, you need a pitch right in the power slot, definitely not low, and it still has to be met on the sweet spot to get that extra charge. My fans in the left-field bleachers had been holding up a "Roofing Ron" sign for quite a while, but I figured it was an inside joke, since that's what I used to do for a living.

HEMOND'S A HE-MAN

Roland Hemond, the White Sox general manager, was a goggle-eyed Comiskey spectator on September 6, 1983, when Kittle's vicious liner off the A's Chris Codoroli rocketed to the roof, just inside the left-field foul pole, bounced once and disappeared into the night.

"I got goosebumps, which didn't happen often," Hemond recalled. "I told the writers, 'We'll warn our maintenance men not to walk on the roof during a game. It isn't safe.' Fans were awed by Ron's power, because they could gauge the distance to the top of old Comiskey's doubled-decked stands.

"You could hear the electricity crackling in the stands when he stepped up to bat, the same way they responded to Frank Thomas in the new park," Hemond noted. "Fans went home comparing the ones Kittle hit with the mighty homers by Dick Allen and Richie Zisk that landed in the center-field bleachers."

Greg Luzinski already had racked up three rooftop homers in 1983 before Kittle connected twice—the second time on September 19 against Minnesota's Mike Walters.

But the Bull's trio of bashes were skyscrapers, in stark contrast to the screaming line drive that inaugurated the muscular rookie into the ranks of the rooftop wrecking crew.

"We had longer to enjoy Bull's three roofers, because they were hit higher and we could admire them from the dugout," said Sox manager Tony La Russa. "Kitty's went down the line and out of here like a cannon shot."

KITTY'S ROOFTOP RAMPAGE

I still feel the same glow when I think back on each of my seven rooftop homers. Maybe the fact I'm proudest of is that Babe Ruth hit the first Comiskey Park roofer, on August 16, 1927, and I got the last one on April 17, 1990, the final season for that wonderful baseball palace. Here's the list of victims, if anyone's keeping score:

No.	Date	Pitcher	Opponent
1.	9 / 6 / 83	Chris Codiroli	Oakland
2.	9 / 19 / 83	Mike Walters	Minnesota
3.	4 / 29 / 84	Al Nipper	Boston
4.	7 / 2 / 84	Dave Rozema	Detroit
5.	8 / 1 / 84	Bob Ojeda	Boston
6.	8 / 8 / 85	Bob Ojeda	Boston
7.	4 / 17 / 90	Rob Murphy	Boston

8

KITTLEISMS AND CONTROVERSY
It's Not All Fun in the Sun

LOOSERS LOSE LESS

One of the first things I learned during my 1982 break-in to the bigs was that the White Sox wouldn't lose many games because they were blinded by flop sweat or hampered by a full load in the pants at crunch time. There were plenty of guys who made sure everyone stayed loose, a role I had played frequently on various clubs while working my way up through the minors. The only thing that really riled me was lack of honest effort. If a young player tightened up or just couldn't seem to shake the jitters whenever the crowd got loud, I tried to find a way to make him smile, or even better, laugh out loud. It was good for him, good for the team and fun for me.

No "No Comment"

I wasn't very quotable during that first series in Texas in 1983. Nobody was thinking about the White Sox winning ugly then. We just needed to start winning any way at all, but it didn't happen until June 23, when we finally got over the .500 mark at 34-33. I was starting to get some recognition around the country by then. It was my 16th homer of the season that helped the Sox beat Minnesota, 7-5 and give us a winning record for the first time. And my three ribbies in that game made me the first in the AL to reach 50.

I had my postgame ad libs already written before the writers reached the clubhouse. A lot of the veterans hadn't felt much like talking in the first few months, so they left it up to me to deal with the media.

When Tony La Russa made me the starting left fielder early in '83, he didn't have to explain it was contingent on my ability to do the job. If you don't perform at the expected level in the majors, they get your butt out of there. You're on the bench one day and back in the minors the next.

Fortunately, I had some quick success. Nobody else on the White Sox was tearing the cover off the ball in the first half of the season. I was hitting pretty decent with some home runs, so I became part of the daily lineup. What happened to get me noticed was that I was doing well, and Greg Luzinski and Carlton Fisk got off to slow starts.

They weren't guys who normally got gabby with the media, especially if they were slumping. Harold Baines was an established star, too, but his postgame comments usually were, "Yes" or "No."

When a writer tried to get the ball rolling by saying, "Harold, you hit that pitch pretty well," he'd reply, "Evidently, because it went out of the park." What I tried to do was feed the media some chatter that would make for good copy—interesting quotes for the next day's sports pages or snappy one-liners for the radio and TV guys. Baseball was fun for me, and I wanted everybody to know that.

BLUE-COLLAR PITCH

There wasn't anybody else feeling very vocal, so most of the spotlight was on me. What the heck, it was something to hang a story on when it looked like the White Sox weren't going anywhere—local boy makes good, flexes muscles, hits long homers and so on. I recall being on Chet Coppock's TV sports show in Chicago and they asked me to show where the strength came from. So I rolled up my sleeve and flexed my bicep. After all those years hammering on iron and steel bars, I was in great shape, and I didn't talk about how much it hurt to stay that way. The fans appreciated my attitude. I kept telling them, "If things don't pan out in baseball, I'll be back to work at my Dad's factory the next morning." They knew I meant it, because I gave what I thought were honest answers to all the questions anybody asked me.

BRITT BURNS UP

Britt Burns, a stoic left-hander with a blazing fastball, blossomed into a winning pitcher while the White Sox were galloping toward their 1983 AL West championship. He's been a long-time admirer of Ron Kittle's ability to hit a baseball and attract an audience.

"If there's one thing Kittle could do better than hit, it was talk," Burns said. "We went to a Chicago fan luncheon in 1983, and they wanted to hear about his rooftop homers. So he got up and talked about them nonstop for 45 minutes. Finally, I had to say, 'Kitty, shut up, so we can get out of here.' That slowed him down for about a minute, but

a fan asked another question and he was off and running again.

"When Kitty came up to the White Sox, he had to learn to be just adequate. His ability to crush the ball was impressive, but he wanted to carry the whole team on his back. Nobody can do that, especially for an entire season. What Ron did was give the Sox an early offensive spark that kept us from falling too far behind."

PEACE, IT'S WONDERFUL

Even after the White Sox really started to roll in midsummer, there weren't a whole lot of talkative people in the clubhouse. Tom Paciorek was feeling a lot better, back to his old lively self when he and La Russa settled their differences. Basically, it came down to accepting the fact that Tony was the boss, something the veterans had to be convinced of before they signed on completely to his computer reports and reliance on statistics and probabilities. A lot of those guys had been schooled by seat-of-the-pants managers like Tommy Lasorda and Don Zimmer, who operated more on experience and hunches.

So, basically it was me, Paciorek and Jerry Koosman who became the unofficial team spokesmen.

Kevin Hickey was a live wire, the goalie in our clubhouse hockey games. He was a Chicago guy and the writers loved his stories about the cut-throat 16-inch softball games in town, but Kevin hurt his shoulder and soon was out for the season.

HICK'S A HIT

Maybe the White Sox had a left-handed version of Ron Kittle in the bullpen, at least during the early stages of 1983. Southpaw Kevin Hickey established himself a year earlier as both a reliable reliever and a fan favorite. A

South Sider himself, the easy-riding Hickey enjoyed telling of his prowess in the Windy City's game, 16-inch, bare-knuckle softball, especially the day he whacked four homers off Mike Royko, the Pulitzer prize-winning Chicago columnist. A sore shoulder shut him down after just 23 relief appearances in '83.

"I threw in the bullpen about 400 times last season, and that's how it happened," Hickey said. "Pitching in Comiskey Park, close to where I grew up, was tremendous, and I was just beginning to feel comfortable. Being in the Sox bullpen and watching for the rest of 1983 was something I'll never forget.

"Ron Kittle hit the longest homer I ever saw in that park, a shot over the left field roof. It was a cold night, about 40 degrees, with the wind blowing in. Whatever role the White Sox needed, he'd be the one to step in and get it done for us."

GIFT OF GAB

George Ofman, a veteran commentator and talk show host on WSCR in Chicago, an all-sports radio station, knows a good interview when he hears one. That's why he, along with most of his colleagues, jockeyed for position around Ron Kittle's locker in the White Sox clubhouse.

"Prior to Ron, baseball's resident character was Bill Lee (an eccentric left-handed pitcher) and they called Lee "Spaceman" for a reason," Ofman said. "Kittle had sort of an Indiana drawl and some people though he was goofy. But that was OK, because he backed up everything he said by hitting some of the longest homers and roof shots ever seen in Comiskey Park. He could always come up with a refreshing, offbeat remark to get a laugh. It was not the usual locker-room cliches.

What, Him Worry?

When somebody asked me a question in my playing days, I gave them an honest answer, without trying to hurt other players' feelings. It wasn't a case of trying to look good at someone else's expense, especially my teammates. I was having a blast, the time of my life. Here was the hometown kid who'd been told not long ago that I would never play ball again for the rest of my life. What did I have to sit there in the White Sox clubhouse and complain about? I was getting the chance to play big-league baseball, my life's ambition.

It made sense that I'd get a lot of coverage in the papers and from radio and TV. I don't think I'm quick-witted, and I didn't have the New York sportswriters to come up with one-liners for me, like they did for Yogi Berra. Usually, I said whatever was on my mind at the moment. It was mostly mild sarcasm, looking for a laugh to break the tension. But the White Sox were trying to drum up publicity for the 50th Anniversary All-Star game, coming up (July 6) in Comiskey Park, and I was leading the American League in home runs, or pretty close to it. Being quotable and available to the media didn't hurt the team—or me.

He's Just Kittleing

Those mammoth home runs created headlines for Ron Kittle, who burst on the Chicago sports scene in 1983, as welcome as a cool breeze off Lake Michigan on a muggy summer afternoon. But unlike William "Refrigerator" Perry," coming to the Bears soon after, Kittle offered more than crowd-pleasing performance on the field and charisma in public. The White Sox rookie had a wry, humorous way of looking at the world and unique ability to explain what he saw. His offbeat quips and comments found their way into print and on the air, although it took a young Sox front-office aide, Dan Evans, to put a label on them. Evans coined the term "Kittleisms" for this rich new vein of humor. For instance:

• *"Everybody kids me about hitting one-handed home runs," Kittle said after bashing one out of Comiskey Park. "At least they have to admit strength is involved. I couldn't do it if I was four foot six, but luckily I'm six foot four."*

• *"I don't do risqué material when I'm talking to groups at banquets or whatever," Kittle insists. "But if the audience is mostly Cub fans, I have a sure-fire way to loosen them up. I tell them, 'Rooting for the Cubs is like having diarrhea all the time. You keep saying, "Aw, shit, not again!"'.' That always gets a big laugh because those fans have suffered through so much with that team. Personally, I'm glad to see the Cubs contending again. I'm a Chicago fan."*

• *When people ask what was his biggest thrill in baseball, Kittle tells them, "My first paycheck." His biggest disappointment? "Paying $20 for an omelet in New York."*

• *Asked how he'd prepared for his 1983 All-Star appearance before a wildly enthusiastic Comiskey Park crowd, Kittle had a classic response: "I'd better be wearing rubber pants."*

• *Kittle on Kittle: "There are only five things I can't do: Figure out my taxes, sing, dance and give birth." And the fifth? "I still haven't decided about that one."*

• *"Ballplayers sometimes do stupid things, like everybody else, but I respect the effort and talent it takes to play professional sports," Kittle responded to a question about use of illegal drugs by players. "For me, the exception is the guys who keep taking drugs after getting second, third, fourth and fifth chances to straighten out. Absolutely, we could tell when they were glassy-eyed and tried to play*

My friends and neighbors appreciated the nationwide publicity I brought to Northwest Indiana.

anyway. If you get caught with drugs, you shouldn't be in this game. When a writer asked if I would have done anything differently in my career, I told him, 'I probably should have gotten high on drugs instead of being injured so much. That way, I would keep getting a pass. They never kick you out of baseball if you're an addict.' I said that kiddingly, but it's a serious knock at the game."

• Kittle's formula for dealing with the media: "They ask me goofy questions and I give them goofier answers."

• On Chicago fans' reaction ("Get him up here!") to Kittle's 50-homer season in 1982 at Edmonton, Alberta: "It's a wonder they ever heard of me. It takes two donkeys and a ski boat to get there."

• Asked why he chose to wear regular glasses instead of contact lenses while playing: "I never was crazy about sticking a finger in my eye."

• *Told that Chicago sportscaster Chet Coppock jokingly suggested a joint investigation by the FBI and the Gary, Indiana, police department if the sensational Sox rookie was not named to the 1983 AL All-Star squad, Kittle replied, "If I don't make it, I'll just go to Great America for three days."*

• *A fast driver, Kittle got to know the traffic cops on Chicago's Dan Ryan Expressway. "When I get pulled over, I give them an autographed ball and Presto! No ticket," he said, quickly adding, "Please tell Mayor Daley I'm just kidding."*

• *Asked if he was surprised that his first 1983 homer was a towering 400-foot blast off Tigers ace Jack Morris, Kittle responded with a question of his own: "Should I be surprised?"*

• *Kittle's reaction to a spring training rumor that the White Sox might farm him out to Denver: "What for? To work on my base-stealing? They say I'd hit 80 home runs in that thin air. I'd rather get one game-winning single for the White Sox than hit 80 homers in Denver."*

• *When Indiana native Kittle was honored by that state's legislature for being named 1983 AL Rookie of the Year, he told Governor Bob Orr, "I'm often asked 'What's a Hoosier?' Haven't figured that out yet, but I know there's a lot of them in Indiana."*

• *Could Kittle have become a left-field Bleacher Bum in Wrigley Field if he hadn't made it to the majors? "I wouldn't have the patience to sit in the stands and watch a baseball game," he replied. "Well, maybe if the ballpark food was good."*

Lots of Luck

Many superstitious players do daily rituals to woo Lady Luck, but the only one I remember from 1983 is that the White Sox thought losing was unlucky. Tony La Russa used to leave vowels out of the names when he wrote his daily lineup cards. Maybe he was just trying to save ink.

I picked up the habit years later, when I was the manager of the Schaumburg Flyers. Sometimes I wrote the names backwards or used red ink for the first letter, green for the second letter and so on. If we won the game, I'd do the same thing the next day.

Maybe that was superstition, but I thought I was just trying to break the monotony. Being around all those funny guys on the White Sox convinced me any way that helped to break the routine of a long season was worth trying. Our '83 bunch was absolutely the loosest group I've ever seen.

Watching TV on a flight to the West Coast, we saw a sign on President Reagan's desk that said, "Great things can be accomplished if you don't mind who gets the credit." I thought, "Hey, that's us." It was the unselfish way we had been playing all season, not worrying about individual stats, and the results began showing up before long. Before I came to the White Sox, the Chicago Bulls had a tough little coach named Dick Motta. He saved that franchise by refusing to back down from anyone, even the team owners, so I really respected him. If not for his determination, Chicago would not even have been in the NBA when Michael Jordan came along in the 1984 draft. And I never forget something I heard Motta say: "I believe in luck. The harder I work, the luckier I seem to get."

HIS SHAER OF CREDIT

Tom Shaer became a sportscaster in Boston, where the fans and media don't just analyze every Red Sox player, every day. They slice and dice them, dissecting the most trivial details of anyone wearing the uniform of the team that arouses more passion and anguish than even the Cubs. Carlton Fisk, a long-time catcher in Fenway Park's outdoor insane asylum, knew the reason why: "They're not the Boston Red Sox. They're the New England Red Sox."

So when Shaer came to Chicago, he brought along the credentials to size up a sports situation with entertaining insight. His take on the 1983 White Sox is proof of that.

"None of these guys hit well for the first few months, so Ron Kittle really lightened the load, coming in to bash some monster homers and drive in runs," Shaer pointed out. "Kittle's power, even before he unloaded those Comiskey rooftop shots, immediately gained respect from the other guys. You know what? He used that fast-quip routine, the Kittleisms and snappy comebacks, to take the pressure off himself. I don't care how much players try to bluff their way through. Everybody on the public performance stage has to have some kind of fear factor.

"You must fear failing in front of all those people. Players use ego and confidence in their ability to overcome it. Talented people find a way to emerge, and Kitty seized the chance in 1983 to step his performance up to another level. While he was at it, he understood there was no harm in being friendly and approachable. The press can't force anybody to speak, but Tony La Russa discovered right away, and the rest of the White Sox sooner or later, that this rookie's good quotes became a sort of safety valve for the rest of them. Instead of blowing up at the writers after a tough loss, they could go sit in the players-only lounge and let Kittle ease the tension by saying something funny.

"Tony's great for young players that way. He's not like Leo Durocher and some of the other Chicago managers who made it hard for rookies to fit in. Kittle was performing at bat, playing a pretty decent left field and kidding in the clubhouse about being so nervous he might have to wear a diaper. People can identify with that."

DON'T QUOTE ME, BUT...

Tony La Russa and others who'd been around the Chicago media scene would give us tips about which reporters you could say things to without your words coming out completely different in print or on the air. White Sox veterans also pointed out the ones you'd better be careful with, because they're more interested in blowing up a story, regardless of the facts.

Rob Gallas (the former *Daily Herald* sportswriter who became the White Sox promotions director until he resigned in 2004) was considered a hatchetman. I got this warning about a couple of other writers: "If you have a drink with them after the game and say something that's supposed to be off the record, you might read it in the sports page the next day." Joe Goddard and Dave Van Dyck (both *Sun-Times*), you had to be a little bit cautious about, but Jerome Holtzman (*Sun-Times* and *Tribune*, now baseball's official historian) was a straight shooter.

LIGHTS OUT IN CLEVELAND

Once in Cleveland's old Municipal Stadium I got called out on a pitch that wasn't even close to being a strike. My neck was hurting worse than usual that day and I wasn't seeing the ball well, but I could hear the ump bellow, "Yer out!" on a ball a foot outside. So I snapped, went back to the dugout yelling, and Tony La Russa interpreted it as uncomplimentary of the sport coat he wore on the bus that morning, or something equally silly. He was not the kind of manager who took guff from anybody, although he could really dish it out to umpires, so he threw me out of the game right away.

I walked up the tunnel to the clubhouse, still mad as hell, punching out every one of those overhead light bulbs as I went. Even with batting gloves on, I cut both wrists, so there was a lot of blood. When I smashed the last bulb, it was pitch dark in the tunnel, but here came Tony charging after me, because he wanted to chew me out some more. I heard Tony trip and fall. He got up, ran to the clubhouse door and pointed his finger at me, hollering louder than ever. At that point, I was trying hard not to laugh out loud.

I'm a very strong man and I could break anything I wanted to, but I never tried to hurt anybody. My temper flared up once in a while, and I simmered down just as fast. So I didn't mind getting reamed out by La Russa, although the Indians sent me a bill for $320 to repair the damage, and I'm sure he told them who did it. Chalk it up to experience, along with a check to pay for letting frustration get the better of me.

GRIN AND BEAR IT

The way it works in the majors, umpires give veterans the benefit of the doubt much more often than rookies. Bull Luzinski and Pudge Fisk kept telling me, "Ronnie, they'll screw you the first few times around the league." What the umpires are really telling the newcomers is, "Sit down and shut up, rookie."

They want to check out your temperament and test you to see if you're a mouthy badass. I never complained much about called strikes a few inches inside or outside, because I swung at a lot of pitches in the dirt or over my head. Some batters beef on every call by the plate umpire, good or bad. That wasn't my style. I was up there to swing, not to serve on a jury. Anyway, when you felt like grabbing the umpire's mask and wringing his neck, it was time to cool it and head back to the dugout. Umps have long memories for anybody trying to show them up.

I got a lesson about the way that works one day in Kansas City when I came to bat with Ken Kaiser umpiring behind the plate. The Royals brought in a right-handed relief pitcher to face me. I believe it was Steve Renko, a big, strapping ex-football player who used to be with the Cubs. As soon as he went into his windup—hadn't even thrown the ball yet—Kaiser yelled, "Ball one!" Pitch was right down the middle.

Same thing on the next pitch, "Ball two!" I was standing there, wondering what gave, but I walked on four pitches. By then, I could tell Renko knew he had ticked off Kaiser sometime before. I stood on the baseline a bit, but Kaiser pointed to first base and told me, "Get over there!" I got. Everybody on both teams was aware the ump was making it clear, "Hey, I run the show here."

A FORD IN HIS FRUSTRATION

A lot of umpires didn't like Tony La Russa's complaints on balls and strikes. He had a real dislike for Dale Ford, and so did the Yankees' Billy Martin. Ford once sued Martin for calling him "a stone liar." I got mixed up in it in Baltimore, when Ford called me out on a pitch way out of the strike zone. I flipped my batting helmet off, so Ford ejected me. Since I was already gone, I decided to get my money's worth by putting the helmet on home plate and smashing it with my bat.

Right away, Tony came roaring out of the dugout, chest to chest with Ford. One thing we could count on from La Russa—he defended his players, right or wrong. I loved him for that.

A few days later, I got slapped with a $500 fine by the commissioner's office. So I sent a note to Bowie Kuhn along with the check: "Dear Mr. Commissioner: Is this tax deductible?" He wrote back, "Sorry, Ron. No way."

TEMPER, TEMPER

Baseball can be very funny when other guys lose their cool and very frustrating when it happens to you. We had a ton of talent on the White Sox, but even the best of them—Fisk, Luzinski, Paciorek, almost everybody except the unflappable Harold Baines—snapped at some point. The rest of us would sit on the bench watching them blow up, enjoying the show, snickering on the inside without laughing out loud. Especially the rookies, because we didn't want the veterans to think we were getting on their case.

Somebody would stomp into the dugout, cussing a blue streak, smash a bat and kick the water cooler. Everybody else had to hold their sides to keep from guffawing.

WILLIE THE WISE

With frayed tempers and flying equipment all around him, Chicken Willie Thompson, the White Sox clubhouse man, sometimes was the court of last resort for angry athletes, cranky coaches and just plain mad managers.

"Everybody else had to pretend they were blind when somebody threw a tantrum in the clubhouse," Thompson said. "Not me. I liked Ron Kittle, because he was fun and a pretty good wrestler, but when he started bashing some empty lockers with his bat because he was in a slump, that was too much. So I went to the bat rack, picked one out and handed it to him. 'You're swinging the bat better in here than you were at the plate, so go on and break this one,' I told him. That got him laughing and a few minutes later, we were eating chicken together."

Yes, We Have No Bonura

For all I knew, the writers were pulling my leg when they asked me what I thought about breaking Zeke Bonura's home run record. Zeke Bonura? Sounded to me like a name they lifted from one of those movies where Burt Reynolds kept outfoxing the rube sheriff, Jackie Gleason. When the TV lights and cameras showed up after I hit my 28th homer of the season on September 2, I got a history lesson. It seemed Zeke Bonura had set the White Sox rookie mark of 27, way back in 1934, so I had just done something worthy of note. I also learned that Zeke was an immobile first baseman who once led the AL in fielding at his position because he couldn't get off a dime, reducing his potential to commit errors.

Since my homer was our only run in a 5-1 loss to Boston that day, I wasn't too impressed. But as usual, I came through for the guys with newspaper deadlines.

"If you think I should be, I'm excited," I said, for the record. "What was that name again? Oh, yeah, Zeke. He was my idol."

Miles of Smiles

I got along with almost everybody by adding a little humor to my dealings with them. I didn't like to lose, but baseball is supposed to be fun. Actually, it's a branch of show business, and if you don't keep the fans entertained, they'll go elsewhere. Bill Veeck knew that and he preached it to the other owners, but a lot of them weren't smart enough to realize he was right. I guess some of Bill's knack for pleasing the crowd rubbed off on me, although I never thought of sending up a midget to pinch hit when I was the manager of the Schaumburg Flyers.

I vented my anger with humor, and it helped me get rid of the frustration when I wasn't helping the team as much as I wanted to. All players have their own methods for dealing with stress, so humor was sort of my medicine. When the writers asked what my weakness was, I used to tell them, "Whatever today's pitcher is throwing." Some guys started drinking when they got into slumps, but I just let it all hang out. It was cheaper than going to see a psychiatrist.

I've always been like that. I didn't bring an extra personality up to the majors with me. It doesn't cost anything to smile at the fans, stop and sign autographs when I can, especially for kids, or hang around the clubhouse an extra few minutes to answer the media questions.

FIGHT, TEAM, FIGHT

Baseball fights are generally just pushing and shoving and cussing back and forth, but they can turn into something nasty if punches begin to fly. With all the money at stake now, players don't want to risk ending their career by getting nailed with a sucker punch.

Sometimes they're pretty funny, like the one between a couple of five-foot-five guys, Harry Chappas and Doug Capilla. That happened on an airplane when I was with the Edmonton Trappers. Our manager, Gordie Lund, was trying to break it up, but the rest of the team wanted to stop him. They were both so aggravating, we hoped they'd kill each other.

Maybe the most ridiculous brawl I ever got involved in was when the White Sox opened the 1989 season in California. It involved Ivan Calderon, who played for us then and just recently passed away. Ivan got hit with a 50-mile-per-hour curve from Bob McClure, the Angels' lefty reliever, and for some reason, he took off his batting helmet to throw it at McClure. But Calderon's thumb got stuck in the earhole, and instead of sailing away, it hit Ivan in the head. He must have thought somebody threw a helmet at him, so he charged the mound.

All of a sudden, this dandy fight breaks out, with guys getting punched. Who's running full speed from the Angels' dugout but the Red Rooster—Doug Rader, one of the roughest, toughest men in baseball.

I tackled Doug and we rolled around on the ground, getting crushed by the pileup on top of us. My glasses fell off, so I yelled, "Don't step on my glasses." At that, the Rooster pulled my helmet off and said, "Kitty, if I'd known that was you, I'd have pulled your pants down and molested you."

At least that's what I think he said. Anyway, everybody started laughing and the fight broke up. They don't always end that peacefully.

9

KITTLE PAYS
THE PRICE
Pain's the Name of My Game

My background was different than most people's, and even most athletes. Not everybody comes back from a broken neck. The medical term is "crushed vertebrae." Spinal fusion surgery in 1978 restored enough mobility for me to swing a bat, run, and do most things other baseball players take for granted. The amount of pain involved in doing them, or even ordinary everyday stuff like mowing the lawn raised a question for me. Did I want to live with that daily struggle and play ball despite it or become a permanent couch potato? For me the answer was easy and loud: "Yes!"

By itself, the neck and spinal problem was manageable. Probably because I went all out in everything I did—and still do—a whole bunch of other injuries happened to me along the way. They included broken thumbs and toes, torn tendons, a cracked collarbone, severe shoulder and knee ailments, nerve damage, a herniated disc, countless bruises and contusions and a mysterious parasitic virus that I picked up in Mexico and can't get rid of.

So you can't blame me for having a different outlook. Pain is always somewhere in my body, and how much I can do just depends on where it shows up. Every day during my career when I woke up and my neck didn't hurt, I felt pretty doggone good about it. Playing on AstroTurf crushed me. Whenever I tried to run on that surface, the neck strain took three or four days to go away when I got back to good old Comiskey Park grass. Only the people really close to me knew it, but a lot of the things I did and said that the fans and media seemed to enjoy were ways to lighten the mood for me, too.

HEAT TOPS HURT

From the bottom of the emotional pit of being told I'd never play baseball again in 1977 to the incredible high of hearing the state legislature proclaim January 10, 1984, as Ron Kittle Day in Indiana took me just over five years. Actually, it was a lifetime, capping a comeback from total despair to recognition as the American League's 1983 Rookie of the Year.

And the neck injury was just the most severe of a string that plagued me constantly; no matter what sport I played. As a tight end on Gary Wirt High School's football team, I broke both thumbs diving for a pass and had to figure out how to insert a fork into the cast on my hand, so I could feed myself. In our family, where I was one of six kids, everybody soon learned you had to fend for yourself and defend yourself.

Growing up that way enabled me to handle whatever problems I faced—and there were plenty—en route to the ultimate thrill. I still get goosebumps recalling the standing ovation I got in Comiskey Park on July 6, 1983, when I was introduced as a member of the AL's All-Star squad. George Brett of the Kansas City Royals whispered to me, "Kitty, that was the loudest, longest ovation I've ever heard." Coming from the man who came close to hitting .400 a few years earlier, that was quite a compliment.

Proud as I was at just being a part of that 50th Anniversary All-Star night in old Comiskey Park, the biggest thrill was when I picked up the sports page the next morning.

There was a quote from my Dad: "Proud? Hell yes, we're proud of Ron." From him, that was the equivalent of a Hall of Fame nomination. We kids never got praise from him just for doing our job, and baseball was my job. Slim Kittle taught me, "If your job is to dig a hole, dig it good and do it right." I knew he always meant what he said. When I was just a little kid, I saw him go out on the back porch of our house, cut the cast off his broken left arm with a steak knife and drive back to his job at the steel mills.

He was a proud man and a strict disciplinarian. I have big paws, but my Dad's forearms were huge, and when he took off his belt, we knew one of us had done something wrong. I knew better than to complain to him when I tore thumb tendons on broken glass in the turf of a minor-league field that used to be a landfill or when I had to leave a winter league in Mexico and come home deathly sick from a parasite that's still in my system to this day. He told all of us, "Get back to work," just like he did, sick or not.

MAN OF IRON—AND STEEL

It was the steel my father put in my backbone that made me shake off the constant pain and find a way to come back in baseball. I'll always be grateful to him for that. Along the way, I got help from a lot of wonderful people, but nobody was with me when I stepped into the batter's box. When the second chance came along, I knew it would be my last shot at a comeback. As a kid, I often imagined stepping up to the plate with a game on the line and getting the winning hit. And not just one of those hump-backed singles, either. I always was a power hitter in my

My family and priest share in Ron Kittle Night at Comiskey in 1983. The backbone my father instilled in me enabled me to excel while playing through pain.

mind, even as a skinny teenager, before I grew to six foot four, 220 pounds. Working 10-hour shifts, lifting iron and steel bars at my Dad's factory gave me the strength to play through those injuries and eventually hit seven home runs on the roof at Comiskey Park.

I never talked much about hurting to the writers or the fans or even the guys I played with. And especially not to my managers and coaches. I didn't want to give them any reasons to keep me out of the lineup, because I needed to play every day. Nobody knew how much pain I was in, although I remember Tom Paciorek asking me, "How can you take all those pain pills and still see straight?"

HOT DOG? NO, HOT PACKS

I wasn't good enough to be a hot dog. For that, you have to be as great as Dizzy Dean, who said, "It ain't bragging if you can do it." That's absolutely true. I was given the gift of being able to hit a baseball, and maybe I should have taken it more seriously. Physically, I was hanging by a thread out there sometimes, but I wanted to get four hits every day. With all those injuries, I knew that couldn't happen.

After getting released by the Dodgers in 1978, many scouts and general managers wrote me off as damaged goods. I had to do twice as well as most other players in the minors to get another look and make it to the big leagues with the White Sox. Possibly, the price my body had to pay for getting there will grow steeper as I get older, but not much. I sacrificed a lot of things along the way to play baseball. Money was not my major interest. I never nickel and dimed any team in contract negotiations. What I wanted was to play ball. The element of competition always has been my definition of a professional athlete.

CAN'T BUG KITTY

Let's get one thing straight—I don't regret any of what I went through to become a big leaguer. That was my No. 1 priority, right from the start. Would I still have traveled that long, hard road if I'd known in advance how much each step would hurt? Absolutely. And would I change anything along the rocky road to Comiskey Park? Absolutely not, except perhaps for stepping on the spider that bit me on the hand soon after reporting to my first spring training camp with the Dodgers. Right away, the swelling went from my wrist all the way up to the shoulder. A doctor lanced it, and pus oozed out of my hand.

It took a week before I could swing a bat. All I could do was eat, so I loaded up my plate. Tommy Lasorda came into the mess hall one day, took a look at what I was putting away and said, "Kid, for somebody who's not playing, you're sure eating a lot."

That sunk into my head, and I never forgot it. When things like that parasite or virus or whatever knocked me out of the box in Mexico, I kept it to myself and always tried to play, no matter what. It's ironic that my knee was swollen up like a soccer ball in that last day in 1983, so I had to sit and watch the White Sox lose Game 4 to end our playoff with the Orioles, but that's life, and baseball is a lot like life.

You have to learn how to handle winning and losing, because there's plenty of both along the way. With everything that happened to me, maybe I should be in a glass case at some medical school. There were times when I took my glasses off because my head hurt so much I couldn't see. Those headaches started when I broke my neck in the minors, so I'd take some Darvon pills and go play.

WALL-OUT EFFORT

Roland Hemond hoped to get a healthy Ron Kittle back for the 1985 season, but the White Sox general manager's optimism soon got another jolt. The injury jinx that had plagued Kittle throughout his career struck again April 20 on a ball hit by the Yankees' Don Baylor. Left fielder Kittle charged hard in pursuit of the Baylor blast, slamming his right shoulder into the bare bricks on Comiskey Park's outfield wall.

"I dislocated the shoulder, but when I picked up the ball and threw to the cutoff man, it popped back into place," Kittle said. "Our trainer, Herm Schneider, came running out while I was looking for my glasses, which flew off when I hit the wall. I'm feeling around in the grass with

my hands when Herm stepped on something and I heard glass shatter. He said, 'Hey, Kitty, I think I found them.'

"Well, I can't see and my shoulder hurts like hell, so I had to leave the game. Jerry Hairston took over in left field. In the same inning, he ran into the wall and hurt himself. The next day, they hung that thick padding all the way around on the outfield walls. It was dangerous out there, and the shoulder that hit the bricks still gives me trouble."

It didn't take long for Hemond to find out that Kittle would play in pain, if he could move at all.

"For two straight winter banquet tours, I'd been hearing Ron talk to our fans about the frustration of having to sit out that last playoff game after Mike Flanagan of the Orioles hit him in the knee with a pitch the night before," Hemond said. "He was hampered by that knee and various other ailments in 1984, but still led the club in homers with 32. A few days after Ron hit the wall in 1985, he talked his way back into the lineup. So I went to the dugout before the game to check things out, and he insisted he was fine. I thought Kittle's jersey looked a little funny, so I asked him to take it off and give me a look at the shoulder. There was a lump the size of a grapefruit. Ron must have been in a lot of pain, but he played and never complained about it. Winning the American League's 1983 Rookie of the Year Award hadn't changed this guy a bit. If anything, he was even hungrier."

MEDICARE ALL-STAR

I had to cope with a lengthy list of injuries during my athletic career. Some of them:

1975: Two broken thumbs playing football at Gary Wirt High School.
1977: Crushed neck vertebrae in minor league game, Clinton, Iowa. Spinal fusion surgery, 1978.

1980: Sliced right thumb tendons on broken glass in minor league field built over landfill.

1983: Severe kneecap cartilage damage, hit by Mike Flanagan pitch in AL playoffs.

1985: Dislocated shoulder, cracked collarbone in collision with Comiskey Park outfield wall.

1987: Nerve damage to neck and skull in freak clubhouse accident.

1988: Broken toe, left foot, hit by Tommy John pitch.

1989: Surgery for herniated spinal disc.

Also, bone chips, inflamed elbow and numerous bruises from being hit by pitches.

THE THIRD STRIKE

When I blacked out at bat during a game in 1991, I went to Dr. Michael Schafer, a trusted friend, at Northwestern Hospital in Chicago. He's been the Cubs physician for years, but he performed the spinal surgery on me in 1978 and he's X-rayed just about every square inch of me. I knew my career was over when Dr. Schafer told me, "Ron, if you keep playing, you'll be in a wheelchair before you're 50."

I believe the bad headaches I kept getting can be traced to nerve damage caused by the broken neck, or maybe to asthma I didn't know I had until after I stopped playing. When I opened a newspaper, I used to sneeze for five or six minutes. That's not because I'm allergic to sportswriters, just some chemical in the ink. But when I was a kid, Dad told me about Wally Pipp, who lost his job at first base for the Yankees in 1925 because he got a headache and took himself out of the lineup for one day. That day turned into 14 years and 2,130 consecutive games for Lou Gehrig. His Iron Man streak lasted until it was broken by Cal Ripken, Jr., later my teammate on the Orioles.

Robin Ventura joins me for Old Timer's Day late in my career. I was fortunate to play alongside a new generation of White Sox stars during parts of the 1990 and 1991 seasons.

When I got hurt in my first minor-league game, Dad wasn't aware the injury was so severe. He kept saying, "Don't forget Wally Pipp." So I didn't whine about how much I was hurting. I kept on playing.

Now, if the pain's really bad, I'll try an afternoon nap with cold pillows. I've slept with every kind of neck brace, support pillow or other new gimmick, but nothing seems to help. My arm was numb until the surgery, although I didn't get a lot of sympathy at home. Dad loved baseball, but he treated me the same as the other kids. There were no favorites in the Kittle household. We were all expected to do our best and constantly pushed to do better. The discipline was tough at times, but I wouldn't have made it to the majors without those constant reminders that quitting was unacceptable.

10

A GRAND SLAM FOR KIDS
Kittle Hits Another Homer

END OF THE LINE

I kept playing until midway in the 1991 season, when my 10 years in the majors ended where I started—with the White Sox. Coming back from all those injuries, I performed most of the time at about 75 percent of my ability. The Sox got me for less than was offered elsewhere, but money never was an issue for me. Every day, I gave the Sox whatever I could on the field. Then something happened that was so scary, I couldn't keep going. I swung at a 2-2 pitch, fouled it off and blanked out, not knowing where I was.

The umpire and the catcher knew something was wrong. Finally, I grounded out, but I knew the trauma caused by the broken neck was affecting my entire body. Maybe I could have stuck around for a couple of years as a designated hitter, but when Dr. Michael Schafer warned me I could end up in a wheelchair, it was time to retire.

It gets a little harder for me to move around now, because I stayed off the disabled list and played hurt. Every day, Laurie yells at me to go to the doctor and get my physical profile reorganized. I tell people that the last time I felt really good I was 12. But I feel a lot better when I see progress in new cancer drugs and treatments, some of them paid for by Indiana Sports Charities. That's why my commitment to this program is set in stone. What I have to do is cut down on giving other people five of six hours of my time every day, so I can spend more with my family. I like coaching my son's Little League team and my daughter's soccer team.

Dad died in 1994, and it took the wind out of my sails. I never told him I loved him until two days before that. We loved each other, but men don't usually say it to each other. Whatever I did was never quite good enough for him, which is fine, because it got me where I am today. You just let it go at that.

A big, tall man, Slim Kittle was down to about 80 pounds and in excruciating pain when they brought him home to die. When Dad first got diagnosed with cancer and emphysema, he asked me to contact Dr. Jack Kevorkian. He was the assisted-suicide doctor from Michigan, who was on his way to jail before I could talk it over with the rest of our family. I never saw my Dad take a pain pill, but he was on a morphine drip at the end.

It was horrible to realize he couldn't do anything to help himself. I've told Laurie I don't want to get to that point. There are worse things than dying. I wanted to be the one everybody else could lean on at Dad's funeral, but for once, I couldn't take it. When I go out, I want people to have a party. My obituary should read: "Ronald Dale Kittle—Dead. House for Sale." You know, something quick and funny.

A LIFE CUT SHORT

In 1979, I played for the White Sox farm team in Knoxville, Tennessee. All of my time and energy should have been focused on cashing in this second chance to restart my career and make it to the big leagues. Most of it was, but something so terrible happened there that it added another dimension to my obligations as a man, not merely as a ballplayer. I had to stop and think about life after baseball, and what I could do to help kids like David.

That's the only name he ever told me. I never knew his last name or how old he was. He lived next door to the house I rented in Knoxville during the season. His parents were drunks, with no health insurance.

Supposedly, David had cancer and needed expensive treatment, but for whatever reason, they tried to kill him. It's tough to avoid getting emotionally drawn to someone in that situation. So I took the kid under my wing, got him haircuts and little treats and fed him at Buddy's Barbeque, a famous Knoxville pigout place. At the time, I was only 19, still a kid myself. I'd give him $5 to wash my car, a blue, souped-up Camaro, or to do odd jobs.

I guess the parents got tired of David's medical problems, so they tried to burn him to death. I came back from a road trip one day and found him dead in my garage. He had hung himself, and he left me a note that said, "I wish you were my big brother. Thanks for taking care of me." Even now, I can still see his face. We called the police, but I couldn't stop thinking I should have done more to help David. For a while, it was hard to go to sleep. I didn't talk about David to the other guys on the team, or even to my Mom and Dad.

Then I got sent to Appleton, Wisconsin, because both catchers on that Sox farm team were injured and they needed me to fill in. It was a good thing for me to get away from that garage in Knoxville. But I started thinking about giving something back to the community. I told my future wife, Laurie, "That kid's tragedy is something I can't tell other people about." Maybe it would have been too hard to put into words. He was a good kid and I tried to make things a little easier for him.

IT'S FOR THE KIDS

What happened to David is one reason why Laurie and I have spent so much time and money over the years trying to help kids who are sick or in trouble. We got involved in many charitable projects, especially Indiana Sports Charities. That's the one I founded and still run to raise money for children's hospitals and research in Northwest Indiana. Our annual golf tournament has contributed a lot for the care and treatment of young people. The first one, in 1989, raised $7,000. In 2003, we distributed a total of $135,000 to five children's hospitals, clinics and research centers. I'm trying to do this the same way I played baseball—keep getting better.

It seems like my wife and I have helped dozens of worthwhile efforts like this, but there's a reason why Indiana Sports Charities stands out. Wherever I traveled in the minors, I still keep in touch with the people I met and their families. Playing ball was fun, but I always took time to say hello to the kids waiting outside the park. To me, it's an obligation all players should meet. That's why I'm pleased to have Ron Kittle listed as founder and chairman of my charity. I have a group of great people like Billy Pierce and many others helping me, and that's how this event works so well. Every year, we're trying to sell more ads for the tournament program, line up prizes and sports memorabilia to auction off and look for more sponsors. I can't do all of those things by myself.

Ron Helps Sam Run

Don Toma, Ron Kittle's junior varsity football coach at Gary Wirt High School in the 1970s, found out that this talented athlete did not feel that his physical ability entitled him to act superior or take advantage of smaller, weaker classmates.

"Ron played end and linebacker for our unbeaten team," Toma said. "What set him apart from other students was the way he got along with everybody and set goals for himself. When he was a sophomore he told me, 'I'm going to be a major league ballplayer.' Since he became famous, I've asked him many times to autograph baseballs or cards for kids, and he never refuses. He goes out of his way to be nice to young players and his old coaches.

"In his student days, Ron played softball in my gym class. There was a kid named Sam who tried to play, but he was mentally challenged, looked undernourished and could hardly hold the bat. Ron was the leader of the guys who yelled, 'Run, Sam!' even if he only got a foul tip. They let him get on base and stand there, beaming with pride. Kittle made sure Sam felt like he was part of the group. So I wasn't surprised when Ron set up the charity that looks after kids. Even after he got hurt and the Dodgers cut him, I knew he'd find a way to make it in the big leagues."

HABIT OF A LIFETIME

I laughed when my friend Don Toma told me, "Ron, you were a good kid in high school, and in some ways, you're still a kid." But I had to admit he was right. Absolutely, it bothers me when grown-ups with everything going for them can't take a minute to help kids. I go to ballparks every year before our golf tournament and get players to sign balls, bats, jerseys and stuff for the auction. Some guys are reluctant or act like it's a pain in the ass. I just tell them, "Sign the damn balls." Most are pretty good about it.

When I was a kid and we'd choose up sides to play ball, my first pick would be somebody who couldn't catch a pop fly and never got a hit. I got in on my share of pranks in school, but if they made somebody feel bad, I felt worse than they did. I used to go visit people in a rehab place where they spent their whole life in a wheelchair or a hospital bed. One guy named Donald never showed any emotion, but I gave him a White Sox jersey and he became a huge Sox fan. He was only 48 when he died.

It's tough seeing people who couldn't talk or move, with drool running down their chin. Some of their parents were embarrassed that they had these children. When I went over there, it was cool to see them coloring pictures of ballgames and feeling better because someone stopped to talk with them. They never thought of me as a jock or a star, and neither did I. Being an ironworker, making money at a good job, would have been fine with me. Doing something for kids has helped me appreciate the good life I've had.

Helping Needs Help

Before my career ended, I was taking a laptop on the road, because the foundation's work went on year-round. I had to contact celebrities for the golf tournament foursomes, set up menus for the banquet, count how many people were signing up and try to keep tabs on everything. You have to fill out a lot of forms just to raise money to give it away. They make it so hard to donate money, but we don't mind making sure it's being done legally.

Indiana Sports Charities started in 1989, when I had back surgery in Chicago. Lying around in bed, I thought about what I could do to give something back to the community. My Dad and my brother-in-law were fighting cancer at the time. So I sat down to dinner with Jerry Reinsdorf and Marv Samuel, founder of Chicago Baseball Cancer Charities, at the Drake Hotel. I told them, "I don't want to be just the front man for a charity with my name on it. I want to get totally involved and make something happen."

And that's what I did. We did it the right way with my charity. Marv called some influential people and said, "Hey, you're helping Ron Kittle out with a charity in Indiana." He kind of strong-armed them into volunteering. Some good friends in this operation have been with me since the beginning. Marv died of cancer a few years later, but his wife and two sons are part of the charity.

GOLF FOR WINNERS

Since 1989, I've been running a golf tournament for Indiana Sports Charities. Every dime we raise goes to care for kids with cancer and other diseases in Northwest Indiana and the Chicago area. Ballplayers, politicians, media people, and celebrities of all kinds contribute their time and money, and my all-volunteer board of directors helps me run the show. Players and coaches sign hats, bats, balls gloves, anything they can, so the people who pay to play golf with them get lots of prizes, a terrific dinner and a good time for their money.

Spending time with young people in hospitals and knowing I can help pay for the research and treatment effort to cure their diseases and lessen their pain gives me the same kind of kick I got from hitting a home run in Comiskey Park, with those White Sox fans going crazy. It's also been wonderful to see such superstars as Michael Jordan, Lou Holtz, Harold Baines, Stan Mikita, Billy Pierce, Mike Ditka, Tommy Lasorda and many others support our tournament and the kids. Anybody who takes a look at me can see that I'm a big, strong man. Those who know me can tell you that I'm an easygoing guy, sort of a gentle giant. I very seldom lose my temper, and that's probably a good thing. Being successful in whatever I do, from mowing the lawn to hitting a baseball, is my nature.

That's why I work so hard to raise every dollar I can for my golf outing. One of the volunteer board members of my charity told me, "Kitty, you're like a bull in a china shop with a baseball bat, except you don't hurt anybody."

A Straight Pitch

Having Billy Pierce's name on the Indiana Sports Charities letterhead opened a lot of doors for us in Illinois. Billy's fans are not just the people who saw him pitch for the White Sox. Everybody he does business with and anyone who knows him is aware that he's a straight shooter. People like him on the committee make my work easier, but I have to do a lot myself. Learning how to raise funds was just the beginning. I contacted all kinds of people, telling them I needed companies and sponsors to support the charity and make the golf tournament a success. I took some courses and figured out how to do it, especially how to pay the bills.

Lou Holtz brought down the house as the speaker at one of our banquets. The place was full of Irish fans, reliving the national championship he won in 1988. Lou had broken his thumb whitewater rafting, but it didn't affect his sense of humor. He told the crowd, "I'm here to practice my after-dinner speaking, so I can have something to fall back on when those Notre Dame alumni run me out of South Bend." But the sore thumb didn't stop him from signing hats, shirts, whatever they handed him. He donated a signed team football and an autographed photo to the auction and when the bidding stalled at $500, he said, "Listen, Ronnie works too hard for this charity to settle for that. How about I throw in two tickets to a football game, plus you come to watch practice and have lunch with the team?" Boom! The bidding went to $2,400, just like that.

ATTACK ON CANCER

I buy game jerseys from the White Sox and other teams and get players to autograph them for the auction. Getting celebrities to play in each foursome takes up a lot of time, and you have to be diplomatic, which sometimes isn't easy for me. But if you yell at them, you lose them, so I rely on my board members to help with that, sending out mailings and other details.

Basically, the money we raise goes to five hospitals: Children's, Munster Community, St. Anthony Medical Center,

Billy Pierce (left), a winning White Sox left-hander who has been instrumental in helping me with my Indiana Sports Charities, greets my parents, James and Dorothy, before a game at Comiskey.

Northwestern Memorial and the University of Chicago Children's. What I do is break it down so donations are spread around to where they came from. Each hospital gets a pretty good chunk of change. What we have done is designate funds for things like the day treatment center at U of C Children's. Kids can go and get cancer treatment in plush recliners and watch TV instead of just sitting there. We put sports memorabilia on the walls, like Walter Payton and Michael Jordan pictures, so they're not so scared. At Northwestern Memorial, we've sponsored research fellowships. These fellowships go toward training the people who will find a cure for cancer one day. We bought a resonator simulator for Munster, only the second hospital in the country to get one. It's a giant machine that directs radiation to one spot and records tumor shrinkage. Where do we get the money for such things?

THE WORD SPREADS

I call up heads of companies and say, "We have 300 golfers coming to our tourney. Do you have 300 miniature bottles of something or 300 combs or 300 whatever that we can put in our gift bags?" The food is great at Briar Ridge CC in Schererville, where we moved after playing the first year at Sand Creek in Chesterton. They have 27 holes at Briar Ridge and we needed the space. Everybody in this area knows what Indiana Sports Charities is. I make it a point, sometimes a rude point, of getting that message out.

Some people respond, "Well, I give to United Way." They don't know United Way sends only 35 cents to charities for every dollar they receive. People get paid for administering that money.

Indiana Sports Charities has an advisory staff. Nobody gets paid, including me. The way I first signed up friends and business owners to help run this operation was by telling them, "I want you on the board. And if you join, it will cost you money." Because of the good people who came on board, 100 percent of what we get goes to help kids. It costs $395 to play in our annual golf event. For that you get a bag with nice gifts and a golf shirt. You eat three fabulous meals—breakfast buffet, lunch on the course, sandwiches, whatever you want, soda, dessert. We have beer carts roaming around and pretty girls selling raffle tickets. Then there's a sitdown steak or chicken dinner after the golf.

Everybody's a volunteer. We had Hooters girls out there the first few years, and they were very cute, but they weren't the most aggressive ticket sellers. The ones with the best personality sell tickets, and that's what this charity is all about—good people caring enough to spend time for a good cause.

REWARDS ARE MANY

A lot of my time and energy goes into planning this tournament. It keeps getting bigger. People have asked me, "What does Ron Kittle get out of all this?" Well, I get to have my kids see their Dad give something back. I get a free golf shirt once in a while. If I wanted to, I could probably make a living out of this, but for me, there's no salary and no perks. I've been asked by hospitals to pitch for them as a fundraiser, because they know I'd work hard enough to earn whatever they paid me. What my board does is work hard to make sure all our money goes to the right places.

I'm getting the executive board to take some of the preparation burden off of me. My wife complains sometimes that it takes up too much of my time. But after 15 years, we've created a pretty good way of running things, so that the golfers get a lot of fun and gifts, door prizes, celebrity autographs and things that make them want to keep coming back every year. I don't

Raising money for charity means wearing a business suit sometimes, not my familiar baseball uniform or golf shirt. I'm in the middle, between Sox announcer Ken "Hawk" Harrelson and the late Oakland A's owner Charles O. Finley.

sleep a lot, so I can get up at night, check my e-mail and see how things are shaping up.

A TIME TO CRY

We created a web page, adding credibility to Indiana Sports Charities. It's the kind of cause that makes people want to pitch in, and I'm proud of what we've done. Back in 1989, when it all began, I had no idea if the back surgery would end my career, so I spread time and energy between trying to play ball and making this charity something that had the potential to help kids fight back against cancer and other diseases. If I could, I'd give their hospitals a million-dollar check every year.

It takes a lot out of you to go into a ward, pick up a little girl and realize she's dying. That gets pretty emotional. And it's really hard not to cry when kids smile at you and you know they may never go home again. My wife, Laurie, lost her sister, Cathy, to cancer. She was a non-smoker, non-drinker with three young kids, and we watched her suffer for five years. I saw my Dad go through the same thing. I don't need personal publicity, but it would be nice if people knew every penny we raise goes to helping sick kids and eventually curing cancer. I'm a very positive person. So I don't get upset, except when rich stars like Barry Bonds won't even sign their name to help kids.

A FATHER'S PRIDE

And since I've spent some time talking about other people, here's what I'd reply if somebody asked me to define Ronald Dale Kittle: A lousy ballplayer who had fun. I was your eager rookie poster boy, just excited to get the chance to play baseball. My Dad used to say, "Boy, after all you've been through, if you ever make it to the big leagues for one at-bat and get called out on strikes, you've had a helluva career. Just tip your cap and walk away."

Slim Kittle was such a fighter that he'd probably have been happier if I swung at that third strike. He didn't take many pitches from anybody and he never showed much emotion, so I didn't learn a lot about how much my career meant to him until he was dying of cancer.

Roland Hemond told me a story that gave me a clue. The White Sox were losing to Kansas City on August 31, 1983, and I hit a three-run homer off Dan Quisenberry to bring us from behind. That was No. 27 on the season, tying me with Zeke Bonura, an old favorite of Sox fans, for the club's rookie record. Roland, sitting next to my Dad, jumped up and hugged him. Dad didn't say anything, but the way he smiled was his version of the standing ovation I was getting from the Comiskey Park crowd.

HOME, SWEET HOME

The White Sox fans were especially good to me, because I lived almost within Bull Luzinski rooftop homer distance of Comiskey Park. Well, not quite, although being able to drive home to Northwest Indiana and sleep in my own bed was a big plus. And having my family and friends in the ballpark to see me playing a major role in the way the White Sox dominated the American League from July on made it even more fun.

I still get together with those hometown and high school friends and coaches. They made Ron Kittle Night at Comiskey Park a huge success on August 29, 1983, raising money for charity by bringing 60 busloads of fans to the game. I don't usually get emotional in public, but I couldn't hide a surge of pride when my Dad, Slim Kittle, shaking off the discomfort from chemotherapy treatments, walked to the mound that night to throw out the first pitch.

NO. 42 IS NO. 1

Right from the start I never had a minute's concern about failing when I put on that uniform as a member of the Chicago White Sox. I chose No. 42 because Jackie Robinson always had been one of my idols. Even as a kid, watching the way he took charge on a ballfield, intimidated pitchers with gung-ho baserunning and always seemed to make the big play with bat or glove, showed me the way baseball should be played.

With Slim Kittle there to remind me every day that nothing less than all-out effort was allowed, I wanted to live up to his expectations, however impossible that might have been. And to this day, I can't stand the chest-bumping, dancing, taunting egomaniacs who turn games into a clown act. My advice to them is the same message I got from my Dad so often: Play, don't bray. The difference is that I listened to him and learned from him.

Just a few decades ago, when the White Sox gave me the second chance I needed, arrogant, ego-driven antics were handled by one's teammates, if not the opposition. If a batter hit a homer and paused at the plate to admire it, the next guy up would need a steel helmet or an entrenching tool, or both. There was a standard of professionalism that was respected and pretty much adhered to on both sides.

Sure, the bench jockeying could get pretty brutal, but virtually all players knew the way a major leaguer was supposed to conduct himself on the field, and they seldom crossed the line.

Not long ago, I heard my old White Sox skipper, Tony La Russa, use that exact phrase to describe the antics of Cubs pitcher Carlos Zambrano. I got the impression that not too many fans recognized Tony's reference to the way it used to be.

A DIFFERENT WORLD

The young guys arriving on the big-time scene now grew up in an age where the old rules of conduct were made to be broken and the old standards just something to be discarded like last year's fashions.

That's the way it is everywhere, in or out of sports.

Maybe so, but that's not the way my wife, Laurie, and I are bringing up our daughter, Hayley, and our son, Dylan. Call us a couple of out-of-touch squares if you disagree, but we believe parents are responsible for setting the limits that give kids the emotional security they need.

My daughter, Hayley, four years old at the time, and son, Dylan, a year old, joined me on the Comiskey Park field for Family Day in 1989.

TIME TAKES TOLL

The funny thing about teaching kids how to hit for 10 years was that it made me a better hitter. I knew more about what I was doing and what pitchers were likely to do. I wanted to keep playing, but things got to the point where my back was fatigued after batting practice and my neck started hurting even more. I had to work out up to six hours a day just to compete in a game and be average, not even good.

The irony of the whole thing is that as the mind gets sharper, the body begins to wear out. It's too bad that some of the really great hitters, like Ted Williams and Joe DiMaggio, couldn't stick around another four or five years as designated hitters. They both would have batted .300 in wheelchairs. If I had kept playing, that's where I would have ended up.

NO MISTAKING HIM

"When Ron Kittle first came to the White Sox, I kept hearing some scouts say he could be pitched to," noted his manager, Tony La Russa.

"Well, you could say that about almost any hitter, and maybe it's true in his case. In theory, a perfect pitch, at the knees on the outside corner, gets everybody out. But baseball is a game of mistakes. When you make one with Kittle at bat, he does some awesome things to it."

"MINE" IS HIS

Among the many memories Dad left me is the name of my clothing company. When I was five or so, he gave me my first baseball glove and wrote "Mine" on it. I remember asking him "Who's Minnie?", but all through the minors and big leagues, when other players wrote their numbers on gloves and spikes, I wrote M-I-N-E on everything, including my jock strap. When I looked at a bat rack full of numbers, I could spot my word right away. That's why the clothing company is called MINE. I also have it on my license plate.

Kind of neat, the way it worked out. I'm not trying to compete with Ralph Lauren, just deliver quality shirts with my label on them. My top priorities are getting my son and daughter through college, so I don't want a regular office job. I never really drew up a game plan for life. When I ran the Kittle's Cages batting clinic and gave lessons to kids, I could have been there

I'm taking aim during batting practice before the 1983 All-Star Game at Comiskey Park. I wrote the word "Mine" on the bottom of the bat, and every other piece of equipment I had during my playing days. Today, my private clothing line is called MINE.

from morning to night. What I need is better computer skills, to simplify all the work I do for Indiana Sports Charities.

Back to Baseball?

It's possible that I'll get back into baseball, maybe as a roving instructor or hitting coach in the minor leagues. It would have to be a situation where I could spend lots of time at home. I had a taste of managing with two teams—the Merrillville Mudcats in Northwest Indiana and the Schaumburg Flyers in the Chicago suburbs. The Merrillville experience would need another book, a big one, or even a Woody Allen movie to put into perspective. It was so bizarre that people still don't believe what went on there. Fortunately, my fans and friends in this area know my version is true, unlike the crook who owned the team.

Merrillville turned out to be a learning experience that cost me $25,000. There were four other teams with us in an independent league—Lafayette, Anderson and East Chicago in Indiana and one from Illinois. The Mud Dogs were run by a guy from Minnesota who turned out to be one of the biggest con men I ever met. They signed players who couldn't play, so I released them, held a midseason tryout and came up with a new team, playing great baseball. One night, the owner backed up a truck to the office, loaded up the computers and other equipment and disappeared. And as if that weren't enough, he accused me of stealing the team's equipment. My salary vanished with him, and there was a month left on the schedule, so I wound up paying the players' salaries, about $400 a month each, out of my own pocket.

Hands-On Manager

"When Ron Kittle managed the ill-fated Merrillville Mud Dogs, they played home games on the high school field there," said Les Grobstein, a veteran Chicago sportscaster. "One time, Kittle got so mad at the umpire that he

stomped out of the dugout and told him, 'I'm not gonna waste any of my pitchers on your strike zone. I'm activating myself right now.' You could get away with anything in that league, so Ron yanked his guy off the mound and went in to pitch for the Mud Dogs himself. As I recall, he hit a few batters, walked a couple and threw some wild pitches.

"But that was vintage Kitty, and the fans loved him for it. One of the funniest men you'll run into, he livened up the clubhouse with a good line for every occasion. When [White Sox general manager] Larry Himes traded him to Baltimore in 1990, Kittle told us, 'I'm glad to get away from that guy. He has the charisma of a pet rock.'"

LIFE'S A BLAST

The thing is, there's nothing I do that I don't get emotionally involved in. That's what happened in 1995, when I walked into the Merrillville fiasco. My intention was to help bring professional baseball into Northwest Indiana in a first-class way. I didn't set out to have a more interesting life than most people. It just sort of worked out that way. Even when the Mud Dogs got into a one-game playoff for the league championship, the plate umpire for that game turned out to be the other manager's brother-in-law. In case you're wondering, we lost.

I still had a sour taste in my mouth about that Merrillville owner not going to jail, but rich guys usually find loopholes. Later, I got talked into managing the Schaumburg Flyers in the Northern League for three years, and I had some fun and some frustration there. The owners figured with my visibility and a brand-new ballpark, they could pack the place, and they turned out to be right. A lot of fans turned to us after they got fed up with the constant complaining by rich, spoiled major-league players.

RON'S FAN CLUB

Wherever Ron Kittle goes, some old friends and fans are sure to show up. So when Kittle began managing the Schaumburg Flyers, 90 miles away from his home base, he wasn't surprised to see a group of his former coaches at Gary Wirt High School waiting to greet him at the ballpark.

"One of us, Ira Judge, had chemotherapy that morning," said Don Toma. "The park was sold out, so we bought bleacher tickets and went to the dugout before the game to say hello to Ron. When we told him we were sitting in the bleachers, he said, 'You old guys will never make it there.' He put us in the owner's skybox. He still respects his elders, even though his Dad was a perfectionist and very tough on him. Whenever we saw him play for the White Sox, some Gary people would be there, rooting for Kittle. It was like a fan convention."

My fans from Northwest Indiana are the most loyal I've ever encountered. This group supported me in the left field bleachers at Comiskey. A group even made their way to Chicago's northwest suburbs when I was managing the Schaumburg Flyers of the Northwest League.

The Right Stuff

Managing, or doing anything that's worthwhile, still comes down to one thing: Do it right. I'm pretty hard on the people I teach or coach, because the best thing for them is to be challenged. I know it makes them better players. What I look for is the right way to make them take that next step. Everybody should question whether they're getting good advice. I could help any big-league organization develop young talent. What concerns me is the way attitudes have changed. Some kids who get $250,000 or more just to sign a contract come into camp saying, "I want to do things my way."

As a player, I was never good enough to satisfy myself. But when I look back at the fun I had and the wonderful friends I've made along the way, it was a trip well worth taking. I could tell a lot more stories about all those good or not-so-good times in the majors and minors, and maybe I will. One of the best human beings I dealt with is Cal Ripken Jr., my former opponent in that unforgettable 1983 AL playoff, later my teammate on the Orioles and always the blueprint for a Hall of Fame baseball player.

His Dad, Cal Ripken Sr., an Orioles' coach, wrote out the lineup card every day and posted it in the Baltimore clubhouse. So I got there early one afternoon, erased Cal Jr. from the lineup, wrote my name in his spot and listed him with the extra players. This was when his consecutive game streak was alive. I just sat there at my locker, watching the players come in and seeing their mouths open wide when they read the lineup.

When Cal Jr. came in, he glanced at it and looked kind of shocked. The whole place was quiet, without the usual music starting up. Finally, somebody went down and whispered in Cal Sr.'s ear. All he said was, "That damn Kittle!" He knew who did it.

Everybody got a good laugh. That's how I'd like to be remembered—"That damn Kittle," who gave the fans a good laugh, gave baseballs a good ride and gave it his best every day.

DATE DUE

#47-0108 Peel Off Pressure Sensitive